Green Bean Salad with Walnut Vinaigrette (left),
Curried Chicken

Green Bean Salad with Walnut Vinaigrette

500g (1lb) green beans, trimmed

½ cup walnut pieces

4 tblspn walnut oil

1 tblspn freshly squeezed lemon juice

½ tspn cracked black pepper

1 Bring a large saucepan of water to the boil, add beans and simmer for 2 minutes, drain.

2 In a large bowl, combine blanched beans and walnut pieces, pour over combined walnut oil, lemon juice and pepper. Toss well and serve.

Serves 4

Smoked Trout and Mango Salad with Chilli Dressing

1 smoked trout, skin and head removed

2 medium ripe mangoes

2 cups coriander sprigs

1 tblspn chilli sauce

1 tspn brown sugar

4 tblspn olive oil

2 tspn freshly squeezed lemon juice

1 Pick out as many bones as possible from the trout, break flesh into small pieces. Peel mangoes, cut flesh from the stone and slice into thin strips.

2 Arrange the pieces of trout, strips of mango and coriander sprigs on a serving plate.

3 In a small bowl, mix together chilli sauce, sugar, oil and lemon juice. Pour dressing over salad and serve.

Serves 4

Alternative starter

Piquant Oysters

Sophistication itself.

24 oysters on the half shell

2 spring onions (scallions), roughly chopped

¼ cup red wine vinegar

1 Place 6 oysters on each of 4 entree plates.

2 Combine spring onions and red wine vinegar in a processor, process until spring onions are very finely chopped.

3 Place about half a teaspoon of sauce on each oyster. Serve immediately.

Serves 4

Smoked Trout and Mango Salad with Chilli Dressing

Pear Souffle

Pear Souffle

3 tblspn butter

3 tblspn plain flour

1½ cups hot milk

½ cup castor sugar

1½ cups drained tinned pears

2 tblspn freshly squeezed lemon juice

3 eggs, separated

1 Melt butter in a large saucepan over moderate heat. Stir in flour and cook for 30 seconds. Remove from heat, gradually stir in hot milk and sugar, return to heat, stir until sauce has thickened, cool to room temperature.

2 Blend or process pears with lemon juice until smooth, stir into sauce. Whisk in egg yolks.

3 Beat egg-whites until soft peaks form, fold into pear sauce mixture.

4 Pour mixture into a 4-cup capacity, greased and collared souffle dish and bake in a moderate oven for 35 minutes or until well risen.

Serves 4

Peppered Garlic Leeks

Classic Bouillabaisse

Rye Bread

Orange Mousse

Alternative Dessert:
*Banana Mousse with
Kiwi Fruit Sauce*

Classic Bouillabaisse

4 tblspn olive oil

2 onions, peeled and sliced

1 large stalk celery, chopped

2 cloves garlic, crushed

1 large carrot, sliced

1 bay leaf

¾ cup dry white wine

410g (13oz) can Italian peeled tomatoes, chopped

1 cup chicken stock

410g (13oz) can tomato puree

250g (½lb) calamari rings

8 green-lipped mussels, debearded and washed

250g (½lb) peeled prawns (shrimp), cooked, peeled, tails intact

1 cooked lobster, flesh chopped, shell reserved

1 Heat the oil in a large saucepan over moderate heat. Add the onion, celery, garlic, carrot and bay leaf, cook stirring constantly for 5 minutes.

2 Add the wine, cook until reduced by half. Add the tomatoes, stock and puree. Simmer for 15 minutes.

*Rye Bread (left),
Classic Bouillabaisse*

3 Stir in the calamari and mussels and cook until mussel shells open — discard any that don't.

4 Stir in the cooked prawns and lobster and cook for 1 minute. Sprinkle with chopped parsley and garnish with lobster tail.

Serves 4

Rye Bread

50g (1¾oz) fresh yeast

2¾ cups lukewarm water (approx)

2 tspn salt

250g (½lb) rye flour

750g (1½lb) plain flour

1 egg, beaten

3 tblspn poppy seeds

1 Dissolve the crumbled yeast in 150ml (¼ pint) lukewarm water, set aside for 10 minutes. Add the salt, rye flour, remaining water and half the plain flour. Stir the dough, then knead in the rest of the flour.

2 Turn dough out onto a lightly floured surface and knead until elastic to the touch, approximately 10 minutes.

3 Place dough in an oiled dish, cover with a wet tea-towel and place in a warm place to rise for 30 minutes.

4 Return dough to a lightly floured surface, knead for a further 3 minutes. Divide dough into six and roll out into sausage shaped lengths. Press three lengths together at one end and plait the lengths. Repeat with remaining three lengths. Place on a greased tray, cover and stand for 20 minutes.

5 Brush with egg and sprinkle poppy seeds on top. Bake in a moderately hot oven for 30-35 minutes.

Makes 2 loaves

Peppered Garlic Leeks

Peppered Garlic Leeks

3 large leeks

4 tblspn olive oil

2 small cloves garlic, crushed

½ tspn cracked black pepper

2 tblspn freshly squeezed lemon juice

1 Discard the green part of the leek, rinse white part thoroughly. Slice leeks into long thin strips.

2 Heat oil in a large frying pan over moderate heat. Add the garlic, cook for 2 minutes.

3 Stir in peppered leeks, stir-fry for 2 minutes, stirring constantly, toss through lemon juice and serve.

Serves 4

Orange Mousse

2 tspn powdered gelatine

2 tblspn water

2 tblspn Cointreau

2 eggs

1 egg yolk

3 tblspn castor sugar

1 cup thickened cream

1 tblspn grated orange rind

¼ cup concentrated orange juice

orange segments and rind to garnish

mint sprigs to garnish

1 Dissolve combined gelatine, water and Cointreau over low heat. Remove from heat and set aside to cool.

2 Beat eggs and egg yolk in an electric mixer on high speed for 5 minutes. Gradually add sugar while beaters are running and continue beating for a further 2 minutes.

3 In a separate bowl, whip cream until soft peaks form. Fold into egg mixture with the orange rind, orange juice and gelatine mixture. Pour mixture into 4 dessert glasses and chill. Decorate with orange segments, rind and mint leaves.

Serves 4

Orange Mousse

Banana Mousse with Kiwi Fruit Sauce

A pretty finale to the lunch. Any left-over ramekins and sauce can be kept in the refrigerator for 2 days.

4 ripe bananas, peeled

juice and grated zest of ½ a lemon

2 tblspn brown sugar

2 tblspn dark rum

300ml (½ pint) low fat plain yoghurt

1 tblspn gelatine

2 eggs, separated

6 kiwi fruit

castor sugar (optional)

1 Place bananas, lemon juice and zest, sugar and rum in a processor, puree until smooth. Scrape into a mixing bowl, add yoghurt and stir to blend.

2 Dissolve gelatine in ¼ cup hot water, stir into banana mixture. Stir in egg yolks. Cover, place in refrigerator.

3 Whisk egg-whites until stiff. When banana mixture is beginning to set, fold egg-whites in lightly but thoroughly. Spoon mixture into six, oiled ramekins, cover and refrigerate until set, about 4 hours or overnight.

4 To make Kiwi Fruit Sauce: Peel kiwi fruit, place in a processor, puree until smooth. Sweeten with castor sugar if desired.

5 Run a knife along the inside of ramekins to unmould, turn out onto dessert plates. Spoon some kiwi fruit sauce around, serve immediately.

Serves 6

Avocado and Smoked Salmon Salad

Rack Ribs

Corn Puffs

Lemon Sorbet with Raspberry Puree

Alternative Starter:
Prawn (Shrimp) and Sugar Snap Pea Salad with Dill Sauce

Rack Ribs

1kg (2lb) American-style pork rack ribs

2 tblspn honey

2 tblspn orange marmalade

1 tblspn tomato paste

1 tblspn vinegar

2 cloves garlic, crushed

2 tblspn redcurrant jelly

1 tblspn Worcestershire sauce

1 Place the ribs in a large baking dish. Combine honey, marmalade, tomato paste, vinegar, garlic, redcurrant jelly and Worcestershire sauce in a medium saucepan over moderate heat. Stir until ingredients are well combined.

2 Brush ribs with the marinade and bake in a moderate oven for 45 minutes, basting regularly.

Serves 4

Rack Ribs (left),
Corn Puffs

Corn Puffs

2 tblspn butter

2 tblspn plain flour

1½ cups hot milk

2 tblspn freshly grated Parmesan cheese

¾ cup corn kernels

3 eggs, separated

1 Melt the butter in a large saucepan over moderate heat, stir in the flour and cook for 30 seconds, remove from heat. Slowly stir in the hot milk, return to heat, cook stirring constantly until sauce thickens.

2 Remove from heat, stir in cheese and corn and cool for 10 minutes. Stir in egg yolks, mix well.

3 Beat egg-whites until soft peaks form, fold into corn mixture. Pour mixture into 4-6, ½-cup capacity, greased and collared souffle dishes. Bake in a moderate oven for 12-15 minutes or until golden and well risen.

Serves 4

Avocado and Smoked Salmon Salad

4 slices smoked salmon, cut into thin strips

2 small avocados, stoned, peeled and thinly sliced

1 cup sliced button mushrooms

¼ cup olive oil

½ tspn brown sugar

2 tblspn freshly squeezed lemon juice

1 tblspn white wine

1 tblspn chopped fresh dill

1 Decoratively arrange salmon, avocado and mushrooms on entree plates.

2 Mix together oil, sugar, lemon juice and wine and pour over salad. Sprinkle with dill before serving.

Serves 4

Alternative starter

Prawn (Shrimp) and Sugar Snap Pea Salad with Dill Sauce

1.5kg (3lb) uncooked prawns

125g (4oz) sugar snap peas, topped and tailed

2 stalks celery, thinly sliced

6 spring onions (scallions), sliced

¼ cup chopped curly-leafed parsley

freshly squeezed lemon juice

4 hard-boiled eggs, roughly chopped

DILL SAUCE

½ cup sour cream

½ cup mayonnaise

¼ cup chopped dill

freshly squeezed juice of ½ a lemon

salt

1 Bring a large pot of salted water to a boil, add prawns, cook until prawns change colour, about 3 minutes. Drain and rinse under cold running water. Peel and devein prawns.

Avocado and Smoked Salmon Salad

2 Plunge sugar snap peas in boiling water, allow water to return to the boil, drain peas immediately. Refresh under cold running water, drain thoroughly.

3 Combine sugar snap peas, celery, prawns, spring onions and parsley in a salad bowl, sprinkle with lemon juice, toss well to mix. Cover and refrigerate until ready to serve.

4 To make Dill Sauce: Combine all ingredients in a small bowl, whisk vigorously until well blended. Season to taste with salt. Cover and refrigerate if made the day before serving.

5 Serve salad cold or at room temperature with the sauce in a separate bowl. Place chopped eggs in a small bowl and pass separately (see note).

Note: As some people have an aversion to hard-boiled eggs, we have opted to serve them separately. Feel free to mix them into the salad though, by all means.

Serves 4 for a main course

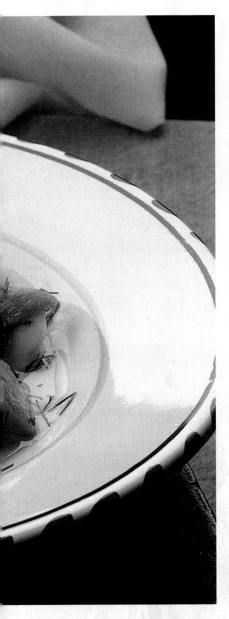

Lemon Sorbet with Raspberry Puree

Lemon Sorbet with Raspberry Puree

1 cup freshly squeezed lemon juice

¾ cup castor sugar

1 tblspn finely grated lemon rind

4 cups water

1 cup lemonade

1½ cups raspberries

1 tblspn raspberry jam

1 tblspn Framboise (raspberry liqueur)

1 Combine lemon juice, sugar, lemon rind and ½ cup of water in a medium saucepan over moderate heat. Stir until sugar is dissolved, remove from heat.

2 Stir in the rest of the water and lemonade and pour mixture into a baking pan, cover and freeze for 4 hours.

3 Break up icicles and return mixture to the freezer. Freeze until set. If using an ice-cream machine, process according to instructions.

4 Blend or process raspberries with the jam and Framboise until smooth. Push mixture through a sieve, discard seeds and serve sauce with sorbet.

Serves 4

Tagliatelle Primavera

Veal with Pepper Cream Sauce

Tomato Basil Salad

Cheese Platter

Alternative Main Course:
Baked Trout Fillets a la Suisse

Veal with Pepper Cream Sauce

8 small veal scallops
flour, for dusting
2 eggs, beaten
1 cup breadcrumbs
90g (3oz) butter
¼ cup dry white wine
1 cup thickened cream
1 tblspn Dijon mustard
1 tblspn green peppercorns

1 Lightly dust veal scallops in flour. Dip in beaten egg and then coat with breadcrumbs.

2 Melt butter in a large frying pan over moderate heat. Cook veal until golden, approximately 2 minutes each side. Transfer veal to a moderately low oven.

3 In a separate frying pan, cook wine and cream over high heat, bring to the boil, reduce heat and simmer for 2 minutes. Stir in mustard and peppercorns, cook until sauce begins to thicken, pour over veal.

Serves 4

Veal with Pepper Cream Sauce

Tomato Basil Salad

2 cups cherry tomatoes, halved

1 cup basil leaves

2 tblspn chopped fresh chives

2 cloves garlic, crushed

3 tblspn olive oil

1 tblspn freshly squeezed lemon juice

1 In a small bowl, combine the tomato halves, basil leaves and chives.

2 Pour over combined garlic, olive oil and lemon juice, toss well and serve.

Serves 4

Alternative main course

Baked Trout Fillets a la Suisse

8 spring onions (scallions), chopped

4 trout (salmon trout, brown trout) fillets, 185g (6oz) each

salt

freshly ground pepper

juice of 1 lemon

⅓ cup chopped button mushrooms

1 cup chopped tomatoes

½ cup chopped continental parsley

½ cup dry white wine

150ml (¼ pint) sour cream

1 Place spring onions in a baking dish large enough to hold fillets in one layer. Season with a little salt. Arrange fillets on top, season with salt and freshly ground pepper, pour over lemon juice, scatter with mushrooms, tomatoes and parsley.

2 Pour over wine, cover with foil, bake in 180°C (350°F) oven until fish is cooked when tested, about 20 minutes. Remove from oven, pour off liquid into a saucepan. Keep fish warm.

3 Add sour cream to fish liquid, bring to a boil and cook until slightly thickened and reduced. Place fish on heated serving plates, pour over sauce, serve hot.

Serves 4

Tagliatelle Primavera

¾ cup cauliflower flowerets

¾ cup broccoli flowerets

250g (½lb) dry tagliatelle

4 tblspn olive oil

2 cloves garlic, crushed

¼ cup red capsicum (pepper), seeded, cut into strips

¼ cup green capsicum (pepper), seeded, cut into strips

¼ cup eggplant (aubergine), seeded, cut into strips

2 tblspn chopped fresh basil

½ tspn cracked black pepper

¼ cup freshly grated Parmesan cheese

1 Bring a large saucepan of water to the boil, add cauliflower, cook for 1 minute. Add the broccoli, cook further 1 minute, drain and refresh under cold water, drain.

2 Cook tagliatelle in boiling water until just tender, drain.

3 In a large frying pan, heat oil over moderate heat. Add garlic, cook for 1 minute.

4 Stir in drained pasta, blanched vegetables, red and green capsicum, eggplant and basil, toss well and serve. Sprinkle over black pepper and cheese.

Serves 4

Tagliatelle Primavera

Cheese Platter

Cheese Platter

300g (10oz) Camembert
300g (10oz) Cheddar
250g (½lb) fruit cheese
200g (6½oz) blue cheese
¾ cup fresh dates
1 pear, sliced, core discarded
1 mandarin, peeled
1 small unsliced loaf

1 On a wooden cheese platter arrange cheeses, dates, pear slices and mandarin segments.

2 Serve with bread slices and/or water biscuits. Serve cheese at room temperature for best flavour.

Serves 4

MEALS IN A MOMENT

These menus are designed for those occasions when you are asked to entertain at short notice. The results are impressive!

Pear and Smoked Chicken Salad

Herbed Veal Schnitzel

Souffleed Parsnips

Berries and Mascarpone

Alternative Dessert:
Peaches with Ricotta and Pecans

Herbed Veal Schnitzel

8 small veal schnitzels

flour, for dusting

2 eggs, lightly beaten

1 cup breadcrumbs

3 tblspn finely chopped fresh herbs

½ cup oil

60g (2oz) butter

lemon slices for garnish

chopped fresh herbs for garnish

1 Trim the veal scallops and dust with the flour. Dip in the eggs and then coat in combined breadcrumbs and mixed herbs.

2 Heat the oil with the butter in a large frying pan over moderate heat. Add veal scallops and cook for 2 minutes each side or until cooked through and golden.

3 Garnish with lemon slices and fresh herbs.

Serves 4

Souffleed Parsnips

5 parsnips, peeled and chopped

¼ cup butter, cut into small pieces

2 tblspn cream

¼ tspn ground nutmeg

1 egg

2 tblspn dried breadcrumbs

2 tblspn grated Parmesan cheese

1 Cook parsnips in a large saucepan of boiling water until tender. Drain and blend or process with the butter until smooth. Stir in the cream, nutmeg and egg.

2 Spoon mixture into a greased ovenproof dish. Sprinkle with breadcrumbs and Parmesan cheese, bake in a moderate oven for 20 minutes or until top is golden and puffed.

Serves 4

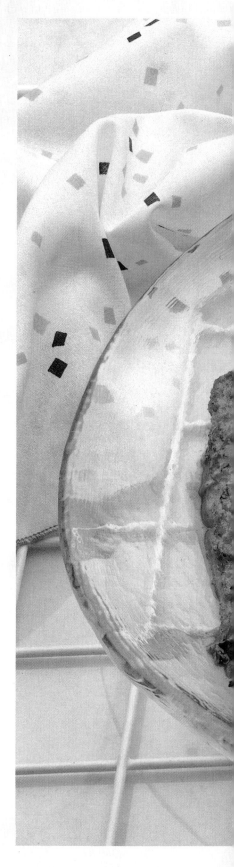

Souffleed Parsnips (top),
Herbed Veal Schnitzel

Pear and Smoked Chicken Salad

2 ripe pears

2 cups smoked chicken, skin removed, cut into strips

2 tblspn butter

2 cups chopped watercress

4 spring onions (scallions), chopped

1 clove garlic, crushed

2 tspn tarragon vinegar

1 tblspn white wine

1 cup thickened cream

1 Slice off two sides of each pear, discarding core. Make cuts vertically in pear without cutting through the top and fan out. Place on entree plate with smoked chicken.

2 To make the dressing: Melt the butter in a medium saucepan over moderate heat, add watercress, spring onions, garlic, vinegar and white wine, simmer for 5 minutes. Stir in the cream, simmer uncovered for a further 10 minutes or until sauce thickens. Blend or process sauce until smooth, pour over salad.

Serves 4

Pear and Smoked Chicken Salad

Berries and Mascarpone

Berries and Mascarpone

2 punnets blueberries

1 punnet strawberries, hulled, quartered

2 tblspn cognac

1 tblspn honey

2 tblspn freshly squeezed lime juice

¼ cup freshly squeezed orange juice

200g (6½oz) mascarpone

broken toffee pieces for garnish

1 Place blueberries in the bottom of 4 serving glass dishes. Top with the strawberries and pour over combined cognac, honey, lime juice and orange juice.

2 Spoon mascarpone on top. Decorate with broken toffee pieces, if desired.

Serves 4

Alternative dessert

Peaches with Ricotta and Pecans

Nothing could be easier.

2 peaches

½ cup ricotta cheese

⅓ cup coarsely chopped pecans

sprigs of mint for garnish

1 Cut peaches in half, remove stones. Cut a very thin sliver from the bottom half, so they will sit flat.

2 Divide ricotta among the 4 peach halves, sprinkle with pecans. Garnish with sprigs of mint.

Serves 4

Spicy Prawns (Shrimps) with Sun-dried Tomatoes

Peppered Eye Fillet with Goat's Cheese

Radicchio and Pinenut Salad

Chocolate Hazelnut Cake with Strawberry Sauce

Alternative Starter:
Tuna Pate

Peppered Eye Fillet with Goat's Cheese and Red Wine Sauce

¼ cup cracked black pepper
750g (1½lb) beef eye fillet, trimmed
60g (2oz) butter
½ cup red wine
2 tblspn redcurrant jelly
1 tspn castor sugar
400g (13oz) goat's cheese, chevre
fresh thyme, chopped

1 Press cracked pepper into the sides of eye fillet, secure meat by tying with string.

2 Melt butter in a large frying pan over high heat. Add the eye fillet and sear well on all sides. Transfer meat to a moderate oven and cook for 30 minutes for medium rare, or longer as desired.

3 Add the red wine, redcurrant jelly and sugar to the frying pan. Simmer until mixture thickens.

4 Slice beef into 4 medallions and top each with a slice of chevre and sprinkle with thyme. Spoon over red wine sauce and serve.

Serves 4

*Radicchio and Pinenut Salad (top),
Peppered Eye Fillet with Goat's Cheese*

Radicchio and Pinenut Salad

2 cups broccoli flowerets

1 radicchio lettuce, shredded

4 tblspn toasted pinenuts

1 red capsicum (pepper), seeded

1 tblspn freshly squeezed lemon juice

¼ tspn cracked black pepper

4 tblspn olive oil

2 tblspn red wine vinegar

1 Bring a large saucepan of water to a boil, add broccoli, cook 1 minute, refresh under cold water, drain. Arrange lettuce on entree plates, top with blanched broccoli and pinenuts.

2 Cut the capsicum into very fine thin strips. Place strips in a cup of cold water and refrigerate for 15 minutes or until they curl.

3 Decorate salad with capsicum curls and dress with combined lemon juice, pepper, olive oil and red wine vinegar.

Serves 4

Spicy Prawns (Shrimps) with Sun-dried Tomatoes

Spicy Prawns (Shrimps) with Sun-dried Tomatoes

3 tblspn olive oil

1kg green king prawns (shrimp), peeled, deveined, tails intact

1 tblspn tomato paste

2 tspn brown sugar

2 cloves garlic, crushed

1 tblspn chilli sauce

1 tblspn chopped coriander

¾ cup sun-dried tomatoes, drained

1 tblspn freshly squeezed lime juice

½ cup snowpea sprouts

1 Heat the oil in a frying pan over moderate heat. Add the prawns and cook for 1 minute each side. Remove prawns with a slotted spoon and set aside.

2 Add the tomato paste, sugar, garlic, chilli sauce and coriander to frying pan and cook for 1 minute.

3 Return prawns to frying pan, add sun-dried tomatoes and toss in chilli sauce and sprinkle with lime juice. Place prawns on to a serving plate.

4 Top with snowpea sprouts to garnish and serve.

Serves 4

Chocolate Hazelnut Cake with Strawberry Sauce

Chocolate Hazelnut Cake with Strawberry Sauce

¼ cup very finely chopped hazelnuts

¼ cup brown sugar

1 pkt rich chocolate cake mix

1 punnet strawberries, hulled

1 tblspn strawberry jam

1 tblspn freshly squeezed lemon juice

1 Grease and line a loaf tin with baking paper. Combine chopped hazelnuts and brown sugar, mix well and evenly sprinkle the base of loaf tin.

2 Mix up chocolate cake according to instructions. Gently pour mixture into pan over the hazelnut sugar mixture. Bake according to instructions. Turn out cake and place a slice on each serving plate.

3 Blend or process strawberries, jam and lemon juice until smooth. Push mixture through a sieve and discard pips. Serve sauce with cake.

Serves 4

Alternative starter

Tuna Pate

200g (6½oz) drained, canned tuna

125g (4oz) unsalted butter, softened (see note)

¼ cup thick cream

½ tspn dry mustard

pinch of cayenne

1 tblspn freshly squeezed lemon juice

2 tblspn brandy

salt

freshly ground pepper

1 Combine tuna, butter, cream, mustard, cayenne, lemon juice and brandy in a processor. Puree until smooth. Season to taste with salt and freshly ground pepper.

2 Transfer to a crock, cover, refrigerate for at least 24 hours before serving, to allow flavours to blend and mellow.

Note: Make sure your butter is really softened, or the pate will be crumbly when set.

Makes 1½ cups

Pears with Prosciutto and Mozzarella Cheese

Pan-fried Tuna with Herb Chilli Sauce

Poached Cucumbers in Yoghurt

French Apple Tarts

Alternative Main Course:
Veal Scallops Provencal

Pan-fried Tuna with Herb Chilli Sauce

4 tblspn butter

4 tuna steaks

¼ cup white wine

¼ cup thickened cream

1 tblspn chopped fresh herbs

1 tspn sambal oelek (chilli sauce)

1 Melt butter in a large frying pan over moderate heat, add the tuna steaks and saute on each side for about 3 minutes. Transfer tuna to a warm plate, cover and set aside in a low oven.

2 Increase heat to high, add the wine to the frying pan, cook for 1 minute, then add the cream, reduce heat and simmer until mixture thickens slightly, about 1 minute.

3 Stir in herbs and sambal oelek and serve sauce with the tuna steak.

Serves 4

Pan-fried Tuna with Herb Chilli Sauce (top), Poached Cucumbers in Yoghurt

Poached Cucumbers in Yoghurt

½ cup dry white wine

¼ cup water

¼ cup vinegar

freshly squeezed juice of 1 lemon

1 clove garlic, crushed

2 tspn brown sugar

1 tblspn dried dill

4 Lebanese cucumbers, thinly sliced

1 cup natural yoghurt

1 Bring the wine, water, vinegar, lemon juice, garlic, sugar and dill to the boil in a medium frying pan over moderate heat. Add cucumbers and poach for 1 minute.

2 Remove cucumbers with a slotted spoon, toss well in the yoghurt and serve.

Serves 4

Veal Scallops Provencal

Imagine yourself in the south of France.

4 thin veal scallops
salt
freshly ground pepper
15g (½oz) unsalted butter
1 clove garlic, finely chopped
1 drained canned pimento, cut into very fine strips
4 black olives, stoned, cut into thin slivers
2 tblspn chopped parsley
15g (½oz) unsalted butter, extra
¼ cup dry white wine
2 tblspn sour cream

1 Season veal scallops with salt and freshly ground pepper.

2 Melt the butter in a heavy-based frying pan, add garlic and pimento, saute for 2 minutes. Add olives and parsley, saute for 2 minutes, remove mixture to a warm plate.

3 Heat the extra butter in the pan, when foam starts to subside, sear scallops quickly, about 30 seconds each side. Turn heat to low, spoon the pimento mixture on top of the meat, add wine to the pan. Cover, simmer for about 6 minutes or until meat is very tender.

4 Remove meat with topping to warmed plates. Reduce wine over high heat, scraping up any browned bits, until syrupy. Pour over scallops and serve immediately, topped with a dollop of sour cream.

Serves 4

Pears with Prosciutto and Mozzarella Cheese

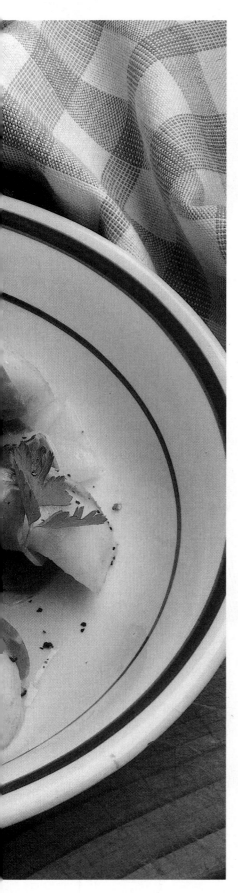

French Apple Tarts

Pears with Prosciutto and Mozzarella Cheese

3 pears, peeled, cored, cut into quarters

freshly squeezed juice of 1 lime

12 slices of prosciutto

100g (3½oz) mozzarella cheese

1 tspn cracked black pepper

4 tblspn olive oil

continental parsley sprigs for garnish

1 Brush each pear quarter with the lime juice and wrap a slice of prosciutto around each one. Arrange three pear quarters on each entree plate.

2 Using a vegetable peeler, peel off slivers of mozzarella cheese and arrange around pears.

3 Sprinkle pepper over the top, drizzle with olive oil and garnish with parsley sprigs.

Serves 4

French Apple Tarts

1 puff pastry sheet, thawed

1 egg yolk, for glazing

1 large green apple, peeled, cored and very finely sliced

1 tblspn honey

1 tblspn castor sugar

whipped cream for serving

1 Cut pastry sheet into 4 squares. Cut a ½cm (1/5in) thick strips from each of the four sides of each square.

2 Brush each square with the egg yolk and place strips on top of each square around the edges to create a border.

3 Brush pastry again with egg and bake in a moderately hot oven for 10 minutes.

4 Arrange the thin slices of apple in the centre of each pastry case, brush with the honey and sprinkle sugar over the top.

5 Bake in a moderate oven for 15 minutes and serve with whipped cream.

Serves 4

Fresh Asparagus Polonaise

Nutty Chicken Breasts

Cheesy Green Bean Salad

*Creamy Vanilla Custard with
Choc-dipped Strawberries*

Additional Side Dish:
Carrot Salad

Nutty Chicken Breasts

4 large single chicken breasts

¼ cup Dijon mustard

2 eggs, lightly beaten

1 cup pecan nuts, finely chopped

1 cup fresh breadcrumbs

½ cup oil

100g (3½oz) butter

1 Spread the mustard over each chicken breast and dip into the beaten eggs.

2 In a large bowl, combine pecan nuts and breadcrumbs, coat chicken breasts and chill for 1 hour.

3 Heat the oil and butter in a large frying pan over moderate heat. Add the coated chicken breasts and fry for 4 minutes each side or until cooked through. Serve immediately.

Serves 4

*Nutty Chicken Breasts (left),
Cheesy Green Bean Salad*

Cheesy Green Bean Salad

500g (1lb) green beans, trimmed

200g (6½oz) mushrooms, sliced

150g (5oz) Gruyere cheese, grated

¼ cup olive oil

4 tspn tarragon vinegar

1 tblspn Dijon mustard

1 tblspn chopped Italian parsley

¼ tspn cracked black pepper

1 Bring a large saucepan of water to the boil, add the beans and blanch for 1 minute.

2 Drain beans and refresh under cold water, drain. Place the beans, mushrooms and cheese in a large bowl.

3 Combine the olive oil, vinegar, mustard, parsley and pepper, mix well, pour over beans, mushrooms and cheese. Toss well and serve.

Serves 4

Additional side dish

Carrot Salad

500g (1lb) carrots, peeled and grated

⅓ cup freshly squeezed lemon juice

pinch of salt

1 tblspn soft brown sugar

½ tspn ground cinnamon

1 Place grated carrots in a salad bowl.

2 Combine lemon juice, salt, brown sugar and cinnamon in a small bowl, stir until sugar has dissolved.

3 Pour over carrots, toss well to mix. Cover and refrigerate until ready to serve.

Serves 4

Fresh Asparagus Polonaise

Fresh Asparagus Polonaise

2 bunches asparagus, trimmed

4 tblspn butter, melted

2 hard-boiled eggs, shelled, chopped

¼ cup thickened cream

¼ tspn nutmeg

capsicum (pepper) strips to garnish

1 Bring a large saucepan of water to boil, add asparagus, cook for 1-2 minutes, drain.

2 Blend or process the melted butter with the chopped egg, cream and nutmeg until smooth. Transfer sauce to a small saucepan and heat through.

3 To serve, spoon over cooked asparagus. Garnish with capsicum strips if desired.

Serves 4

Creamy Vanilla Custard with Choc-dipped Strawberries

Creamy Vanilla Custard with Choc-dipped Strawberries

1 punnet strawberries

100g (3½oz) dark chocolate, melted

4 egg yolks

4 tblspn castor sugar

1½ cups cream

3 tspn vanilla essence

1 Holding the stalk of the strawberry, dip each into the melted chocolate to cover three-quarters of the strawberry. Place chocolate-dipped strawberries on baking paper and allow to harden at room temperature.

2 To make the custard: Beat egg yolks with the sugar for 2 minutes. Scald the cream in a medium saucepan, slowly pour into egg mixture, whisking vigorously. Add the vanilla essence and return mixture to the saucepan. Stir over low heat until thickened, without boiling, cool slightly.

3 Pour into serving glasses and serve with strawberries.

Serves 4

Brie with Raspberry Coulis and
Brioche Toasts

Julienne Vegetable Frittata

Warm Lettuce Salad with
Mushrooms and Mandarines

Summer Fruit Fool

Alternative Main Course:
Spaghetti with Cold Fresh
Tomato Concasse

Julienne Vegetable Frittata

3 tblspn oil

1 onion, peeled and sliced

i0 asparagus tips

2 zucchini (courgette), cut into thin strips

1 red capsicum (pepper), seeded, cut into thin strips

8 eggs, lightly beaten

¼ cup grated Parmesan cheese

½ tspn salt

¼ cup light sour cream

1 Heat the oil in a large non-stick frying pan over moderate heat. Add the onions, asparagus, zucchini and capsicum strips, cook for 3 minutes.

2 Whisk eggs together with the Parmesan cheese, salt and sour cream and pour over the vegetables. Reduce heat to moderately low, cook frittata for about 10 minutes, or until top is almost set.

3 Transfer frying pan to a moderate grill and cook until top is set. Cut frittata into wedges to serve.

Serves 4

Warm Lettuce Salad with Mushrooms and Mandarines (top), Julienne Vegetable Frittata

Warm Lettuce Salad with Mushrooms and Mandarines

4 tblspn olive oil

2 cloves garlic, crushed

1 cup sliced large mushrooms

3 cups shredded lettuce

1 tblspn freshly squeezed lemon juice

½ cup mandarine segments, drained

1 Heat the oil in a large frying pan over moderate heat. Stir in the garlic and mushrooms, cook for 2 minutes.

2 Stir in the shredded lettuce, lemon juice and mandarine segments, toss well and serve.

Serves 4

Alternative main course

Spaghetti with Cold Fresh Tomato Concasse

A taste of summer.

500g (1lb) spaghetti

4 small tomatoes, chopped

2 tblspn tomato puree

2 tblspn chopped fresh basil

¼ tspn chilli flakes (optional)

2 tblspn olive oil

1 tblspn red wine vinegar

salt

freshly ground pepper

1 Bring a large pot of lightly salted water to a boil. Add spaghetti. Cook until al dente.

2 In a pasta bowl, combine tomatoes, tomato puree, basil, chilli flakes if used, oil and vinegar. Mix well to combine, season to taste with salt and freshly ground pepper.

3 When pasta is cooked, drain and add to bowl. Toss well to coat. Serve immediately.

Serves 4

Brie with Raspberry Coulis and Brioche Toasts

1 punnet fresh raspberries

200g (6½oz) wedge Brie cheese

1 round plain brioche

8 dried figs, sliced

whole raspberries, to decorate

1 Blend or process raspberries until smooth, push through a sieve, discard pips.

2 Cut the Brie into 4 equal wedges and place on 4 entree plates. Spoon a little raspberry puree next to the cheese.

3 Slice the brioche very finely and toast under a moderate grill until golden on each side.

4 Garnish Brie and raspberry coulis with a few slices of brioche toast, dried figs and whole raspberries, if desired.

Serves 4

Brie with Raspberry Coulis and
Brioche Toasts

Summer Fruit Fool

4 egg-whites

1 cup sugar

150ml (¼ pint) cream

1 punnet strawberries, hulled, sliced

½ cup blueberries

¼ cup raspberries

1 Using an electric mixer, beat egg-whites until soft peaks form. Slowly add sugar in an even stream, beat for 3 minutes further or until light and glossy.

2 Beat cream until thickened and fold into egg-white mixture. Gently stir in strawberries, blueberries and raspberries and serve.

Serves 4

BARBECUES WITH STYLE

Barbecues are the epitome of relaxed entertaining, so add some style to your next outdoor feast with these tempting menus.

Spinach Creams with
Tomato Sauce

Salmon with Lime Butter
Baste

Broad Bean and Tomato Salad

Caramel Mousse

Alternative Side Dish:
Broccoli and Cauliflower
Stir-fry with Garlic Mayonnaise

Salmon with Lime Butter Baste

90g (3oz) butter
1 clove garlic, crushed
¼ cup freshly squeezed lime juice
2 tspn grated lime rind
2 tspn grated lemon rind
1 tblspn dry white wine
2 tspn honey
1 tblspn chopped dill
4 x 200g (6½oz) salmon fillets

1 Melt the butter in a small saucepan over moderate heat. Stir in the garlic and cook for 1 minute. Add the lime juice, lime rind, lemon rind, wine and honey, mix until combined. Stir in the dill and brush baste over each fillet.

2 Barbecue salmon for 3 minutes each side, basting regularly with lime butter.

Serves 4

Broad Bean and Tomato Salad

2½ cups broad beans

¼ cup black olives, pitted and sliced

2 cups Italian tomatoes, halved (or use cherry tomatoes)

2 tblspn chopped fresh parsley

¼ cup olive oil

2 cloves garlic, crushed

½ tspn pepper

2 tblspn red wine vinegar

1 Bring a large saucepan of water to the boil, add broad beans, blanch for 2 minutes, drain and refresh.

2 In a medium bowl, combine broad beans, olive slices, tomatoes and parsley.

3 Pour over combined olive oil, garlic, pepper and vinegar and toss well.

Serves 4

Alternative side dish

Broccoli and Cauliflower Stir-fry with Garlic Mayonnaise

2 tblspn good quality egg mayonnaise

1 clove garlic, crushed

¼ cup olive oil

1 clove garlic, extra, crushed

2 cups broccoli flowerets

2 cups cauliflower flowerets

1 Combine mayonnaise with garlic, whisk until smooth.

2 Heat the oil in a large frying pan, add extra garlic, saute for 1 minute. Add broccoli and cauliflower flowerets, saute until vegetables are crisp-tender. Remove to a heated serving dish.

3 Spoon mayonnaise over vegetables, serve immediately.

Serves 4

*Broad Bean and Tomato Salad (top),
Salmon with Lime Butter Baste*

39

Spinach Creams with Tomato Sauce

3 tblspn butter
1 onion, peeled and chopped
1 tblspn chopped mixed herbs
3 eggs
½ cup milk
¾ cup cream
½ tspn ground nutmeg
1 bunch spinach, cooked, chopped and drained
½ cup tomato puree
¼ cup red wine
2 tblspn sweet fruit chutney
2 tblspn water

1 Melt butter in a large saucepan over moderate heat. Stir in the onion and herbs, cook for 2 minutes.

2 Mix the eggs, milk, cream and nutmeg together in a blender or food processor until combined. While motor is running, add spinach and onion mixture, process for a further 1 minute.

3 Grease 4 timbale tins and pour spinach mixture into each and cover with foil. Place timbales in a baking dish filled with 2cm (¾in) of hot water and bake in a moderate oven for 30 minutes.

4 In a medium saucepan, combine tomato puree, red wine, chutney and water, bring to the boil and cook until slightly thickened. Serve with timbales.

Serves 4

Spinach Creams with Tomato Sauce

Caramel Mousse

Caramel Mousse

2½ tspn gelatine

135g (4½oz) sugar

5 eggs, separated

2 tblspn castor sugar

300ml (½ pint) double cream

1 Dissolve the gelatine in 3 tablespoons cold water in a double saucepan over simmering water.

2 Dissolve the sugar over low heat with 2 tablespoons water. Bring to the boil and cook until syrup turns a rich brown caramel. Remove from the heat, cool for 5 minutes. Gradually add 4 tablespoons of water, stirring to dilute the caramel. Be careful, as caramel may spit. Wait about 5 minutes, then stir the gelatine into the hot caramel.

3 Whisk the egg yolks with the castor sugar until light and creamy, add the caramel and continue to whisk until mixture is fluffy. Whip the cream and fold into the mixture, then whisk the egg-whites until fluffy and fold into the caramel. Spoon into serving glasses, top with extra cream and serve.

Serves 4

Cheese Roulade with Neufchatel Cheese

Mixed Seafood Skewers

Endive and Avocado Salad

Pawpaw (Papaya) and Cherry Salad with Cherry Brandy

Alternative Main Course:
Barbecued Stuff Snapper

Mixed Seafood Skewers

12 scallops, deveined

12 green king prawns (shrimp), deveined, peeled, tails intact

2 salmon fillets, cut into 1½cm (5/8in) cubes

60g (2oz) butter

3 tblspn freshly squeezed lemon juice

1 clove garlic, crushed

¼ tspn ground black pepper

2 tblspn chopped fresh chervil

2 tblspn chopped fresh dill

2 tblspn chopped fresh thyme

1 Thread 3 scallops onto 4 skewers. Thread 3 prawns onto 4 skewers and thread 3 pieces of salmon onto 4 skewers.

2 Melt butter in a small saucepan over moderate heat, stir in lemon juice, garlic and pepper. Brush each skewer with butter lemon mixture.

3 Sprinkle chervil over scallops, sprinkle dill over prawns and sprinkle thyme over salmon. Barbecue kebabs for 2 minutes each side.

Serves 4

Endive and Avocado Salad (top),
Mixed Seafood Skewers

Endive and Avocado Salad

2 avocados, pitted, peeled and sliced

1 endive lettuce

2 cups watercress sprigs

1 tspn Dijon mustard

3 tblspn freshly squeezed lemon juice

¼ cup olive oil

1 tblspn finely chopped fresh tarragon

1 Arrange avocados, endive and watercress sprigs decoratively on serving plates.

2 Dress with combined mustard, lemon juice, olive oil and tarragon.

Serves 4

Alternative main course

Barbecued Stuffed Snapper

1 whole snapper (red mullet, black sea bass), about 1.5kg (3lb), cleaned and scaled

STUFFING

1 tblspn unsalted butter

8 spring onions (scallions), chopped

1 clove garlic, crushed

1½ cup chopped fresh continental parsley

60g (2oz) ham, chopped

¼ cup fresh breadcrumbs

2 tpn Dijon mustard

1 To make stuffing: Melt butter in a frying pan, add spring onions, garlic, parsley, ham and breadcrumbs. Saute for 2 minutes, or until spring onions have softened. Stir in mustard, mix in well.

2 Spoon stuffing into the snapper cavity, wrap snapper securely into a double thickness foil. Cook on the barbecue, on a rack over coals, for 60 minutes, turning once. Check for doneness. Serve immediately.

Serves 4

Cheese Roulade with Neufchatel Cheese

Cheese Roulade with Neufchatel Cheese

5 eggs, separated

2 tspn Dijon mustard

125g (4oz) freshly grated Parmesan cheese

40g (1½oz) fresh breadcrumbs

FILLING

250g (½lb) strawberry neufchatel cheese, softened

1 cup sliced pimento

1 Line a Swiss-roll tin with greased baking paper.

2 Beat egg yolks with mustard until light. Fold in the cheese. Beat the egg-whites until stiff. Fold into the yolk mixture, then fold in the breadcrumbs. Spread over the prepared tin and bake in a moderate oven for 15 minutes.

3 Run a knife around the edge of the tin and turn out onto a sheet of baking paper. Cool to lukewarm, then roll up the roulade, using the paper to help. Keep rolled and when cool, cover and refrigerate.

4 Unroll the roulade. Spread a layer of neufchatel over surface. Scatter the pimentos over the top, reroll and slide onto a serving platter. Keep in a cool place until ready to serve. Served sliced.

Serves 4

Pawpaw (Papaya) and Cherry Salad with Cherry Brandy

Pawpaw (Papaya) and Cherry Salad with Cherry Brandy

1 pawpaw (papaya), seeded

1½ cups cherries

2 tblspn finely chopped fresh mint

3 tblspn cherry brandy

1 Using a melon baller, scoop out 3 cups of pawpaw flesh. Place in a large bowl with cherries and mint, pour over cherry brandy and toss.

2 Cover and refrigerate for 30 minutes before serving.

Serves 4

YOUR 'ENTERTAINING' STORE CUPBOARD

When you're short of time in the kitchen, it's a help to have all the basic ingredients to hand. Why not stock up with these staples so that you'll always have what's required when you need it. If you buy a little often, you'll hardly notice any extra costs.

Biscuits and Grains

Biscuits for cheese
Corn chips for dips
Breadcrumbs
Plain flour
Self-raising flour
Wholemeal flour
Pasta and noodles —
spaghetti, fettucine,
macaroni, fussili, spinach
pasta, egg noodles
Plain long-grain rice
Basmati rice
Arborio rice
Bulgur
Tortillas
Poppadoms

Sauces and Condiments

Tomato ketchup
Tabasco sauce
Chilli sauce
Sambal oelek (Chilli paste)
Angostura bitters
Mayonnaise
Dijon mustard
Wholegrain mustard
Dry mustard
Horseradish
Olive oil
Walnut oil
Vegetable oil
Vinaigrette
Pesto
Soy sauce
Tamari
Peeled Italian tomatoes
Tomato paste
Chicken, beef and
vegetable stock cubes
Vinegar, white, red wine,
white wine, tarragon and
cider
Worcestershire sauce
Sun-dried tomatoes
Salt, cooking salt, sea salt
Peppercorns
Cracked black pepper
Herbs and spices
Curry Powder
Chutney
Gherkins

Frozen Foods

Home-made stocks
Fresh breadcrumbs
Peas
Broad beans
Butter
Margarine
Bacon
Pancetta
Filo pastry
Puff pastry
Bread rolls
Orange juice concentrate

Canned Foods

Anchovies
Crabmeat
Salmon
Prawns (shrimp)
Tuna
Corn
Artichoke hearts
Pimentos
Bamboo shoots
Hearts of palm
Beans
Olives
Water chestnuts
Consomme
Fruits

For Baking

Sugar, granulated, brown,
castor, icing sugar
Vanilla essence
Corn syrup
Maple syrup
Honey
Jam, jelly, preserves
Desiccated coconut
Unsweetened cocoa
powder
Instant coffee powder
Dark Chocolate
Raisins
Nuts — almonds, pecans,
peanuts, walnuts
Dried apricots
Oil — vegetable, peanut
Vegetable shortening —
copha
Gelatine
Bi-carbonate of soda
Baking soda
Baking powder

Wines and Spirits

Brandy
Coffee Liqueur
Dry red wine
Dry white wine
Orange liqueur (Grand
Marnier, Cointreau)
Rum
Dry sherry
Vermouth
Vodka

Cheeses

Cheddar
Parmesan
Gruyere
Blue-vein cheese
Camembert
Brie
Cream cheese
Feta
Cottage cheese
Mozzarella

8-DO-AHEAD MENUS

DO-AHEAD MENU I

Avocado and Palm Heart Salad

Seafood Pot Pie

Watercress Salad with Croutons

Blackberry Mousse

Alternative recipe for Blackberry
Mousse:
Heart Shapes with Passionfruit
Sauce

Preparing ahead is time-saving and takes a lot of the worry out of entertaining. These complete menus enable you, the hostess, to enjoy the occasion too.

DO-AHEAD MENU VI

Tomato Thyme Soup

Spatchcock with Wild Rice
Stuffing

Lettuce Salad with Lemon
Vinaigrette

Oranges in Red Wine Syrup

Alternative recipe to Spatchcock
with Wild Rice Stuffing:
Boned Chicken stuffed with
Herbed Zucchini (Courgettes)

DO-AHEAD MENU II

Mozzarella Ham Parcels with
Antipasto

John Dory and Vegetable
Casserole

Persian Rice

Blinis with Strawberry Topping

Alternative Starter:
Orange and Avocado Salad

DO-AHEAD MENU IV

Chilli Lime Marinated Scallops

Chicken and Mushroom Parcels

Broccoli Snowpea Salad

Hazelnut Creams with
Apricot Sauce

Alternative to Hazelnut Creams:
Gooseberry Mousse

DO-AHEAD MENU VII

Smoked Fish Pate

Veal Scallops with Bacon and
Leek Sauce

Creamy Whipped Potatoes
and Cream

Strawberry and Almond Creams

Alternative recipe to Veal
Scallops:
Beef Daube

DO-AHEAD MENU III

Gravadlax

Chicken Breasts with Garlic
Cream Sauce

Parmesan Potatoes with Oyster
Mushrooms

Sabayon with Berries

Alternative to Chicken Breasts
with Garlic Cream Sauce:
Roast Sirloin with Herb Sauce

DO-AHEAD MENU V

Mozzarella and Quail's Egg Salad

Pork Fillet with Curry Sauce and
Mango Accompaniment

Zucchini (Courgette) Pudding

Fresh Fruits with Vanilla Cream

Additional recipe:
Parsnip and Capsicum
(Pepper) Slaw

DO-AHEAD MENU VIII

Smoked Trout and Asparagus
Terrine

Lamb Cutlets with Blue Cheese
and Pears

Orange and Fennel Salad

White Chocolate Mousse

Alternative to Lamb Cutlets:
Chicken Saute with Dill and
Lemon Sauce

Avocado and Palm Heart Salad

Seafood Pot Pie

Watercress Salad with Croutons

Blackberry Mousse

Alternative Dessert:
Heart Shapes with
Passionfruit Sauce

Watercress Salad with Croutons

3 cups watercress sprigs
¼ cup toasted pinenuts
45g (1½oz) butter
6 slices bread, crusts removed, cut into 1½cm (5/8in) squares
4 bacon rashers, rind removed
¼ cup red wine vinegar
¼ cup olive oil
1 tspn brown sugar
3 tblspn thickened cream

1 Arrange watercress and pinenuts in a salad bowl.

2 Melt butter in a medium saucepan over moderate heat. Add the bread and fry until golden, remove with a slotted spoon. Add bacon to pan, fry until crisp.

3 Sprinkle croutons and crumble bacon over salad and dress with the combined red wine vinegar, oil, sugar and cream.

Serves 4

Watercress Salad with Croutons (top),
Seafood Pot Pie

Seafood Pot Pie

2 cups dry white wine

500g (1lb) scallops, deveined

3 tblspn butter

1 green apple, peeled, cored and chopped

1 onion, peeled and chopped

1 large carrot, peeled and chopped

½ red capsicum (pepper), seeds removed, chopped

½ cup chicken stock

½ cup cream

2 tblspn flour

¼ cup milk

350g (11oz) green prawns (shrimp), peeled, deveined

½ cup corn kernels

1 sheet ready-rolled puff pastry

1 egg-white

1 Place the wine in a large, deep frying pan, bring to the boil over moderate heat, reduce by a third. Add scallops and simmer until they just turn opaque. Remove with a slotted spoon, set aside. Reserve the scallop wine stock.

2 Melt the butter in a large saucepan over moderate heat. Add the apple, onion, carrot and capsicum, saute for 5 minutes. Pour in the reserved scallop stock, chicken stock and cream. Simmer mixture for 5 minutes.

3 Mix the flour with the milk to form a smooth paste. Stir paste into simmering stock mixture, stir until sauce thickens. Stir in the reserved scallops, the prawns and corn. Pour mixture into a 23cm (9in) ovenproof pie dish.

4 Trim pastry to fit pie and place on top of filling. Make a few slits in the pastry and brush with egg-white. Bake in a moderate oven for 30 minutes.

Serves 4

Avocado and Palm Heart Salad

Avocado and Palm Heart Salad

400g (13oz) tin palm hearts, drained, thinly sliced

1 medium avocado, peeled, stoned and sliced lengthwise

2 tblspn freshly squeezed lemon juice

75g (2½oz) piece of Parmesan cheese

4 tblspn chopped walnut halves

1 red capsicum (pepper), seeded, cut into thin 1cm (½in) strips

2 tblspn freshly squeezed lemon juice, extra

4 tblspn walnut oil

¼ tspn paprika

1 tblspn chopped fresh dill

1 Arrange the slices of palm hearts and avocado on entree plates, sprinkle with the lemon juice.

2 Using a potato peeler, pare the Parmesan cheese into curling slivers, and place on salad. Add the walnuts and capsicum strips.

3 In a small bowl, combine extra lemon juice, walnut oil and paprika and pour over salad. Sprinkle with the chopped dill.

Serves 4

Blackberry Mousse

500g (11b) fresh or frozen blackberries

¼ cup castor sugar

2 tblspn freshly squeezed lemon juice

2 tspn freshly grated lemon zest

2½ tspn gelatine, dissolved in 3 tblspn cold water

¾ cup thickened cream

2 egg-whites

2 tblspn sugar, extra

1 Place the blackberries in a medium saucepan over moderate heat. Stir in the sugar, lemon juice and lemon zest, mix well and gently simmer mixture for 10 minutes.

2 Push mixture through a sieve and return to saucepan. Stir in the gelatine and dissolve over low heat, but do not boil! Remove from heat, set aside to cool to room temperatue.

3 Beat the cream with an electric mixer until soft peaks form, then fold into cooled blackberry mixture.

4 Beat egg-whites with the extra sugar until fluffy, fold into blackberry cream mixture.

5 Spoon mixture into four serving glasses, decorate with extra whipped cream, blackberries and mint sprigs if desired.

Serves 4

Blackberry Mousse

Heart Shapes with Passionfruit Sauce

Even people who do not like yoghurt will love this dessert; they would never guess it is the main ingredient in this luscious treat.

2 egg-whites

440g (14oz) thick-set yoghurt (see note)

castor sugar to taste

PASSIONFRUIT SAUCE

75g (2½oz) sugar

freshly squeezed juice of ½ a lemon

10 passionfruit

1 Whisk the egg-whites until stiff peaks form, fold in yoghurt. Add castor sugar to taste. Line 4 individual heart shaped moulds with holes in the bottom with damp cheese cloth, divide the yoghurt mixture among the moulds. Place moulds on a plate and leave to drain in the refrigerator overnight.

2 To make the Passionfruit Sauce: Dissolve the sugar in 75ml (2½ fl oz) water over low heat. Bring to a boil, remove from the heat. Stir in lemon juice.

3 Cut passionfruit in half, scoop out the insides, place in a processor. Process for 15 seconds, just long enough to detach the yellow membranes from the seeds. Rub through a sieve, pressing out all the juice. Mix into the syrup, allow to cool to room temperature. Cover and refrigerate.

4 Turn hearts out onto 4 dessert plates. Pour the passionfruit sauce around hearts and serve immediately.

Note: This recipe works very well with low fat yoghurt, which makes it a slimmer's delight!

Serves 4

Mozzarella Ham Parcels with Antipasto

John Dory and Vegetable Casserole

Persian Rice

Blinis with Strawberry Topping

Alternative starter:
Orange and Avocado Salad

Persian Rice

2 cups basmati rice
2 egg yolks
⅓ cup butter
1 tblspn chopped coriander
1 tspn cracked black pepper
⅓ cup water

1 Cook rice in boiling water for 5 minutes. Drain and mix egg yolks through the rice and spoon mixture into a buttered, ovenproof dish.

2 Melt the butter in a medium saucepan over moderate heat, stir in the coriander, pepper and water and pour mixture evenly over the rice. Bake in a moderate oven for 35 minutes.

Serves 4

Persian Rice (left), John Dory and Vegetable Casserole

John Dory and Vegetable Casserole

4 tblspn oil

500g (1lb) John Dory (flounder) fillets, cut into big slices

1 onion, peeled and sliced

½ red capsicum (pepper), seeded and cut into thin strips

3 tblspn butter

½ cup dry white wine

½ tspn cracked black pepper

½ cup sour cream

4 large yellow squash, sliced

2 cups broccoli flowerets

1 Heat the oil in a large frying pan over moderate heat, add the fish slices and cook gently for 1 minute. Remove fish with a slotted spoon and set aside.

2 Add the onions and red capsicum strips to the pan and cook for 2 minutes. Remove from pan with a slotted spoon and set aside.

3 Add butter to the pan with the wine, pepper and sour cream, bring to the boil and reduce by a third. Pour sauce through a sieve, return to pan.

4 Add the squash and broccoli to the pan, cook for 1 minute. Add the fish slices, onion and capsicum strips to the pan. When ready to serve, warm through gently.

Serves 4

Mozzarella Ham Parcels with Antipasto

Mozzarella Ham Parcels with Antipasto

200g (6½oz) mozzarella cheese

4 square slices ham

4 spring onions (scallions)

12 sun-dried tomatoes

¾ cup stuffed olives

1 clove garlic, crushed

½ cup olive oil

1 tblspn chopped fresh basil

1 tspn cracked black pepper

1 tblspn freshly squeezed lemon juice

1 Cut the mozzarella into 2cm x 7cm (¾in x 2¾in) lengths, or just longer than the width of the ham. Roll each slice of cheese in the ham and tie a spring onion around each one.

2 Place a parcel on each entree plate, then arrange sun-dried tomatoes and olives on the plate and dress antipasto with combined garlic, olive oil, basil, pepper and lemon juice.

Serves 4

Alternative starter

Orange and Avocado Salad

1 curly endive, washed

2 oranges, peeled and segmented

1 ripe avocado, peeled, stoned and cubed

2 tblspn chopped spring onions (scallions)

2 cloves garlic, crushed

¼ tspn cracked black pepper

1 tblspn freshly squeezed lemon juice

4 tblspn freshly squeezed orange juice

3 tblspn oil

1 Arrange curly endive, orange segments and avocado cubes in a salad bowl. Sprinkle with spring onions (see note).

2 Combine garlic, pepper, lemon juice, orange juice and oil in a screwtop jar, shake until well combined.

3 Pour dressing over salad, toss well to coat. Serve immediately.

Note: If desired, this salad can be made ahead of time, but do not dress salad until ready to serve. Simply sprinkle avocado cubes with a little freshly squeezed lemon juice, cover bowl and refrigerate for up to 4 hours.

Serves 4

Blinis with Strawberry Topping

Blinis with Strawberry Topping

1 cup milk, warmed

1 tspn castor sugar

15g (½oz) yeast

3 eggs, separated

½ cup sour cream

1¼ cups plain flour

2 tblspn butter

1 punnet strawberries, hulled and quartered

1 cup strawberries, hulled, extra

3 tblspn Cointreau

ice-cream to serve

1 Combine warm milk, sugar and yeast and stand for 10 minutes. Whisk together the egg yolks and sour cream and combine mixture with yeast mixture.

2 Whisk in the flour, cover with a damp tea-towel and allow to stand in a warm place for 1 hour.

3 Beat egg-whites until light and fluffy and fold into yeast mixture.

4 Heat the butter in a large frying pan, add tablespoons of mixture to pan and fry for 1 minute each side. Drain on paper towels and top with strawberry quarters.

5 To make strawberry sauce: Blend or process the extra strawberries with Cointreau until smooth, push through a sieve and pour over blinis. Serve with ice-cream if desired.

Serves 4

Gravadlax

*Chicken Breasts with Garlic
Cream Sauce*

*Parmesan Potatoes with Oyster
Mushrooms*

Sabayon with Berries

Alternative Main Course:
Roast Sirloin with Herb Sauce

Chicken Breasts with Garlic Cream Sauce

4 double chicken breast fillets

flour for dusting

4 tblspn butter

2 cloves garlic, crushed

150ml (¼ pint) chicken stock

100ml (3 fl oz) dry white wine

150ml (¼ pint) thickened cream

1 Lightly coat the chicken fillets in flour. Melt the butter in a large frying pan over moderate heat, add chicken fillets and cook for about 2 minutes each side or until nearly cooked through. Transfer fillets to a warm oven.

2 Add the garlic to the frying pan and cook for 1 minute. Add the stock and wine and deglaze the pan.

3 Stir in the cream and simmer until sauce reduces and thickens slightly, about 3 minutes. Serve sauce over fillets.

Serves 4

*Chicken Breasts with Garlic Cream Sauce (left),
Parmesan Potatoes with Oyster Mushrooms*

Parmesan Potatoes with Oyster Mushrooms

100g (3½oz) butter

*400g (13oz) baby potatoes, peeled,
thinly sliced*

100g (3½oz) oyster mushrooms

2 tblspn olive oil

½ cup packaged, grated Parmesan cheese

1 Melt butter in a large frying pan over moderate heat. Add the potatoes, cook, stirring constantly, for 7 minutes or until tender.

2 Add mushrooms, olive oil and Parmesan cheese, toss well and serve.

Serves 4

Roast Sirloin with Herb Sauce

1.5kg (3lb) sirloin roast, preferably aged sirloin

salt

freshly ground pepper

2 tblspn Dijon mustard

HERB SAUCE

¾ cup firmly packed continental parsley leaves

½ cup firmly packed fresh coriander leaves

6 sprigs dill

6 spring onions (scallions), roughly chopped

½ cup olive oil

yolk of a hard-boiled egg

1 large clove garlic

2 tblspn freshly squeezed lemon juice

1 tspn Dijon mustard

salt

freshly ground pepper

1 Season sirloin roast with salt and freshly ground pepper to taste, brush with mustard. Place in a preheated 160°C (325°F) oven for 90 minutes, or until a meat thermometer inserted in the thickest part of the roast shows an internal temperature of 71°C (160°F). Remove from oven and allow to stand for 15 minutes. If desired cool beef to room temperature.

2 Meanwhile, make Herb Sauce: Combine all ingredients in a processor, puree until smooth. Season to taste with salt and freshly ground pepper.

3 Carve meat into thin slices. Serve warm or at room temperature with the Herb Sauce in a separate dish. If desired, the meat can be refrigerated up to 4 days.

Serves 6-8

Gravadlax

Gravadlax

750g (1½lb) skinned and boned fresh salmon

2 cups rose wine

rind of 1 orange

rind of 1 lime

½ cup walnut oil

2 tblspn chopped fresh coriander

1 tblspn cracked black pepper

2 tblspn chopped fresh dill

4 tblspn coarse sea salt

8 tblspn brown sugar

1 Remove the skin from the salmon and lie flat in a dish. Combine the wine with the orange and lime rind and pour over the salmon. Cover and refrigerate for 1 day.

2 Remove the salmon from marinade and pat dry with a paper towel. Brush the oil over salmon and sprinkle with half the combined coriander, pepper, dill, salt and sugar.

3 Turn salmon over onto a large sheet of foil and sprinkle the other half of the herbs over salmon. Seal foil and refrigerate for a further 2 days before serving.

Serves 4

Sabayon with Berries

Sabayon with Berries

3 egg yolks
3 tblspn castor sugar
2 tblspn Cointreau
1 tspn gelatine
½ cup cream, thickened
1 cup strawberries, hulled and sliced
¾ cup blueberries
icing sugar

1 Place egg yolks, sugar and Cointreau in a medium bowl set over a saucepan of hot water, (not boiling). Whisk mixture until thick, about 3 minutes, remove from heat.

2 Dissolve the gelatine in 3 tablespoons cold water, then set over simmering water until clear. Whisk the dissolved gelatine into egg mixture and continue to whisk until mixture cools.

3 Fold the cream into the sabayon and serve with strawberries slices and blueberries, dusted with icing sugar.

Serves 4

Chilli Lime Marinated Scallops

Chicken and Mushroom Parcels

Broccoli Snowpea Salad

Hazelnut Creams with Apricot Sauce

Alternative Dessert:
Gooseberry Mousse

Chicken and Mushroom Parcels

4 tblspn butter

4 single chicken breasts

400g (13oz) mushrooms, sliced

4 large rounds thinly sliced ham

12 sheets filo pastry

½ cup oil, for greasing

1 Melt the butter in a large frying pan over moderate heat, add the chicken fillets and mushrooms, cook the chicken on each side for 4 minutes. Transfer chicken and mushrooms to paper towels and drain.

2 Place the mushrooms on top of each chicken fillet, and wrap a slice of ham around each fillet. Wrap each parcel with three sheets of greased filo pastry to form a pillow shape.

3 Place parcels on a greased oven tray and cook in a moderate oven for 30 minutes.

Serves 4

Chicken and Mushroom Parcels (top), Broccoli Snowpea Salad

Broccoli Snowpea Salad

4 cups broccoli flowerets

2 cups snowpeas, trimmed

⅓ cup pinenuts, toasted

¼ cup salad dressing

1 Bring a large saucepan of water to the boil, add the broccoli and cook for 1 minute.

2 Add the snowpeas and cook for 30 seconds. Drain vegetables and refresh under cold running water.

3 Toss the broccoli, snowpeas and pinenuts in the salad dressing and refrigerate until ready to serve.

Serves 4

Chilli Lime Marinated Scallops

Chilli Lime Marinated Scallops

24 scallops, rinsed and deveined

12 cooked king prawns (shrimp), peeled, deveined and cut into 2cm (¾in) lengths

¼ cup freshly squeezed lemon juice

4 tblspn freshly squeezed lime juice

2 tspn sambal oelek (chilli sauce)

rind of 1 lime, cut into strips

2 tblspn chopped dill

4 tblspns olive oil

1 In a medium bowl, combine the scallops and prawns with the lemon juice, lime juice, chilli sauce, lime rind, dill and oil, mix well; cover and refrigerate for 2 hours, stirring occasionally.

2 Serve on a small plate and garnish with fresh dill if desired.

Serves 4

Hazelnut Creams with Apricot Sauce

Hazelnut Creams with Apricot Sauce

1 cup dried apricots, soaked in water overnight

1½ cups milk

60g (2oz) ground hazelnuts

3 egg yolks

¼ cup brown sugar

10g (⅓oz) gelatine powder, mixed with 4 tblspn cold water

1 Place the apricots and water in a blender or food processor and puree until smooth. Refrigerate until ready to serve.

2 Place the milk and the ground hazelnuts in a large saucepan, slowly bring to the boil, reduce heat and simmer for 10 minutes.

3 Cream the egg yolks and sugar together until pale. Whisk in the simmering milk and return to the saucepan. Stir mixture over low heat until custard begins to thicken. Pour mixture through a sieve and allow to cool.

4 Dissolve the gelatine over low heat and stir into the cooled hazelnut custard mixture. Stir in the cream and pour mixture into four, lightly oiled ramekins and chill until set.

5 Turn out moulds, serve with the apricot sauce and garnish with fresh fruit if desired.

Serves 4

Alternative dessert

Gooseberry Mousse

This is an extremely rich dessert, so serve very small portions.

2 cups gooseberries, fresh or frozen and defrosted (see note)

300ml (½ pint) cream

¼ cup castor sugar

1 Cook gooseberries in ½ cup of boiling water until tender. Allow to cool. Puree in a processor.

2 Whip cream in a bowl until stiff, fold in pureed gooseberries and sugar. Cover and refrigerate until ready to serve.

Note: If gooseberries are difficult to obtain, raspberries, blackberries or strawberries can be substituted.

Serves 6

Mozzarella and Quail's Egg Salad

Pork Fillet with Curry Sauce and Mango Accompaniment

Zucchini (Courgette) Pudding

Fresh Fruits with Vanilla Cream

Additional Side Dish:
Parsnip and Capsicum (Pepper) Slaw

Pork Fillet with Curry Sauce and Mango Accompaniment

3 tblspn oil

2 x 400g (13oz) pork fillets

2 tblspn mild curry powder or paste

1 tspn ground cumin

1 tspn ground coriander

1 cup cream

1 cup mango flesh, chopped into small pieces

1 small onion, peeled and chopped very finely

2 tblspn chopped fresh coriander leaves

1 tspn chilli sauce

1 Heat the oil in a large frying pan over moderate heat, add the pork fillets and sear well on all sides. Transfer pork to a moderate oven and cook for 30 minutes.

2 Pour off any excess fat from frying pan and return to heat. Add the curry powder, cumin, coriander and cream, simmer mixture until reduced by a third.

3 Slice fillets and pour over sauce. Serve with combined mango, onion, chopped coriander and chilli sauce.

Serves 4

Pork Fillet with Curry Sauce and Mango Accompaniment (left),
Zucchini (Courgette) Pudding

Zucchini (Courgette) Pudding

1 cup zucchini (courgette), grated

½ cup sour cream

1 onion, grated

½ tspn salt

4 eggs

125g (4oz) cream cheese, softened

½ cup grated mature cheese

1 Blend or process zucchini, sour cream, onion, salt, eggs, cream cheese and mature cheese until smooth.

2 Pour mixture into four greased and lined, ½-cup capacity ramekins. Bake in a moderate oven for 30 minutes, turn out and serve.

Serves 4

Parsnip and Capsicum (Pepper) Slaw

An unusual and delicious salad.

2 parsnips, peeled and very finely julienned

1 green capsicum (pepper), seeds removed, cut into 0.5cm (¼in) cubes

1 red capsicum (pepper), seeds removed, cut into 0.5cm (¼in) cubes

¼ cup roughly chopped walnuts

½ cup sour cream

mixed lettuce leaves

⅓ cup Walnut Dressing (recipe follows)

½ cucumber, peeled and very thinly sliced

1 Combine julienned parsnips in a bowl with capsicum and walnuts. Add sour cream and toss well to coat.

2 Place lettuce leaves in a shallow salad bowl, add dressing, toss well to coat. Arrange cucumber slices in a circle around the edge, mound parsnip slaw in the centre, Serve cold or at room temperature.

Serves 6

Walnut Dressing

2 large cloves garlic, crushed lightly with the blade of a knife

2 tblspn red wine vinegar

¼ cup walnut oil

2 tblspn olive oil

salt

freshly ground pepper

1 Combine all ingredients in a screwtop jar, shake until well combined. Check seasoning.

Makes about ½ a cup.

Mozzarella and Quail's Egg Salad

Mozzarella and Quail's Egg Salad

2 cups watercress sprigs

¼ cup thickened cream

3 tblspn mayonnaise

2 tblspn salad dressing

300g (9½oz) mozzarella cheese

8 quail's eggs, hard-boiled, shelled and halved

1 Arrange the watercress sprigs around the edge of each entree plate. In a medium bowl, combine the cream, mayonnaise and dressing.

2 Cut the cheese into batons approximately 2cm (¾in) in length and toss in the mayonnaise dressing. Arrange the coated cheese batons and quail's eggs in the middle of the plate and garnish with a curl of red capsicum if desired.

Serves 4

Fresh Fruits with Vanilla Cream

Fresh Fruits with Vanilla Cream

2 mangos

2 kiwi fruit

1 punnet strawberries

1 cup whipped cream

½ cup sour cream

2 tblspn icing sugar, sifted

4 tspn vanilla essence

1 Decoratively arrange the fruit on each serving plate.

2 Place the whipped cream in a medium bowl, fold in the sour cream, icing sugar and essence and refrigerate until ready to serve.

Serves 4

Tomato Thyme Soup

Spatchcock with Wild Rice
Stuffing

Lettuce Salad with Lemon
Vinaigrette

Oranges in Red Wine Syrup

Alternative Main Course:
Boned Chicken Stuffed with
Herbed Zucchini (Courgette)

Lettuce Salad with Lemon Vinaigrette

2 cups assorted lettuce leaves, torn into bite-size pieces

⅔ cup snowpea sprouts

1 lemon, segmented, cut into small pieces

1 tblspn lemon rind, cut into thin strips

4 tblspn olive oil

2 tblspn freshly squeezed lemon juice

2 tblspn honey

¼ tspn cracked black pepper

1 Arrange the lettuce leaves with the snowpea sprouts, lemon segments and rind decoratively on a serving plate.

2 Pour over combined olive oil, lemon juice, honey and pepper, just before serving.

Serves 4

Spatchcock with Wild Rice Stuffing

2 tblspn butter

4 tblspn apricot jam

1 tblspn honey

4 spatchcocks

4 tblspn oil

¾ cup fresh breadcrumbs

1 clove garlic, crushed

¾ cup cooked wild rice

1 tblspn dry herbs

½ cup tinned apricots, drained, finely chopped

1 Melt the butter in a medium saucepan over moderate heat, stir in the jam and honey and stir until dissolved. Brush each spatchcock with the apricot glaze.

2 Heat the oil in a large frying pan over moderate heat. Stir in the breadcrumbs and garlic, cook for 1 minute. Add the rice, herbs and apricots, mix well and fill each spatchcock cavity with the stuffing.

3 Bake in a moderate oven for 40 minutes, basting spatchcocks regularly with apricot glaze.

Serves 4

Spatchcock with Wild Rice Stuffing (top),
Lettuce Salad with Lemon Vinaigrette

Boned Chicken Stuffed with Herbed Zucchini (Courgette)

Ask your butcher to bone chicken for you; some will even stuff the bird if you bring in your own stuffing. It's best to ask in advance.

1 x 1.5kg (3lb) chicken, boned

fresh coriander mayonnaise to serve (recipe follows)

HERBED ZUCCHINI (Courgette) STUFFING

345g (11oz) zucchini (courgette), unpeeled, grated

salt

1 tblspn olive oil

2 tblspn finely chopped onion

30g (1oz) unsalted butter

1 tblspn finely chopped fresh dill

1 tblspn finely chopped fresh chives

60g (2oz) pistachio nuts, coarsely chopped

½ cup cooked brown rice

1 egg, lightly beaten

salt

freshly ground pepper

freshly squeezed lemon juice

1 To make stuffing: Place zucchini in a colander, sprinkle with salt. Allow to drain for 15 minutes. Heat oil in a heavy-based frying pan over moderate heat, add onion, saute until soft, about 5 minutes. Add butter, dill, chives and pistachios, saute 2 minutes. Squeeze courgettes by the handful until dry, stir into the frying pan. Cook for 3 minutes, stirring constantly. Transfer mixture to a bowl, mix in rice and beaten egg. Season to taste with salt and freshly ground pepper and lemon juice.

2 Lay boned chicken on a flat surface, skin side down. Lightly season inside with salt and freshly ground pepper. Spread stuffing evenly over chicken, roll up into a sausage shape. Tie securely with string.

3 Cook in a 190°C (375°F) oven for 1 hour and 30 minutes. Remove from oven, allow to cool to room temperature. Wrap in foil and refrigerate overnight. Cut into 2.5cm (1in) slices to serve (see note). Serve with fresh coriander mayonnaise in a separate bowl.

Note: This chicken can be served warm, although it will be easier to slice when cold. If desired it can be sliced cold and reheated very gently in a warm sauce of your choice.

Serves 4

Fresh Coriander Mayonnaise

½ cup tightly packed coriander leaves

3 egg yolks

2 tblspn freshly squeezed lemon juice

½ tspn salt

½ tspn dry mustard

freshly ground pepper

1-1½ cups olive oil

1 Place coriander leaves in a processor, chop finely. Add egg yolks, lemon juice, salt, mustard and pepper, process until well combined.

2 With machine running start pouring oil into the bowl, first very slowly, after the first half a bit faster (see note). Scrape mayonnaise into a serving bowl and keep refrigerated until ready to serve.

Note: You may not want to use all the oil; stop adding when the consistency seems right.

Makes about 1½ cups

Tomato Thyme Soup

Tomato Thyme Soup

4 tblspn butter

2 onions, peeled and sliced

2 tblspn finely chopped fresh thyme

1 leek (white part only), sliced

2 stalks celery, sliced

3 cups tinned tomatoes and juice

2 cups chicken stock

⅓ cup thickened cream

thyme sprigs to garnish

Oranges in Red Wine Syrup

1 Melt the butter in a large saucepan over moderate heat, add the onion, thyme, leek and celery and cook for 2 minutes.

2 Add the tomatoes and their juice, and the stock, bring soup to the boil, reduce heat and simmer for 30 minutes. Blend or process soup until smooth.

3 Return to the saucepan and heat through. Stir in the cream and ladle soup into four soup dishes. Garnish with thyme sprigs if desired.

Serves 4

Oranges in Red Wine Syrup

2 cups red wine
4 tblspn redcurrant jelly
½ cup castor sugar
4 large navel oranges, peeled and segmented

1 Place the wine, redcurrant jelly and sugar in a medium saucepan over moderate heat. Bring mixture to the boil, reduce heat and simmer for 10 minutes or until sauce thickens slightly.

2 Pour over orange segments and serve.

Serves 4

Smoked Fish Pate

Veal Scallops with Bacon and Leek Sauce

Creamy Whipped Potatoes and Carrot

Strawberry and Almond Creams

Alternative Main Course:
Beef Daube

Veal Scallops with Bacon and Leek Sauce

4 tblspn olive oil

1 cup chopped bacon, rind removed

1 leek (white part only), thinly sliced

1 tspn freshly grated lemon rind

2 cloves garlic, crushed

¼ tspn cracked black pepper

8 veal scallops

½ cup plain white flour, seasoned

½ cup dry white wine

1 cup stock

1 Heat the oil in a large frying pan over moderate heat. Add the bacon and leek, cook for 3 minutes, stir in the lemon rind, garlic and pepper. Remove from frying pan and set aside.

2 Coat the veal scallops in seasoned flour, and add to the frying pan. Brown veal on both sides. Remove veal and keep warm in a low oven.

3 Deglaze pan with the wine and stock, scraping up the meat bits on the bottom of the pan.

4 Pour through a sieve and return sauce to the pan. Simmer until sauce thickens slightly. Stir in bacon and leek mixture and pour sauce over veal scallops.

Serves 4

Veal Scallops with Bacon and Leek Sauce (left), Creamy Whipped Potatoes and Carrot

Beef Daube

750g (1½lb) round steak, all visible fat removed, cut into 2.5cm (1in) cubes

125g (4oz) smoked speck, cut into 0.5cm (¼in) cubes

1 onion, peeled and sliced

185g (6oz) black olives

1 punnet cherry tomatoes

MARINADE

300ml (½ pint) dry white wine

1 tblspn brandy

1 tblspn olive oil

1 onion, peeled and sliced

2 cloves garlic, crushed with the blade of a knife

zest of half an orange

2 sprigs fresh oregano

6 parsley stalks

1 To make marinade: Combine all ingredients in a large bowl. Stir to mix well.

2 Add meat, combine well. Cover and refrigerate overnight. Drain meat, reserve marinade liquid, discard vegetables and herbs.

3 Place speck in a heavy-based casserole, saute over medium heat until fat runs freely, about 10 minutes. Raise heat, add onion, saute until golden brown, about 10 minutes. Remove onion and speck from casserole.

4 Raise heat to high, sear pieces of meat, in 3 batches, until brown on all sides. Remove browned pieces while cooking a new batch. Return all browned pieces to the casserole with the onion and speck. Add olives and reserved marinade.

5 Bring to a simmer, cover casserole and cook in a preheated 160°C (325°F) oven for 2 hours or until meat is tender. Check liquid level from time to time. If daube becomes too dry, add a little hot water.

6 Ten minutes before daube is cooked, stir in cherry tomatoes, allow to heat through. Serve hot, straight from the casserole.

Serves 4

Creamy Whipped Potatoes and Carrot

3 large potatoes, peeled, cut into 2cm (¾in) cubes

1 large carrot, peeled, cut into thin slices

2 tblspn butter

4 tblspn cream

1 tblspn chopped chives

1 Boil potatoes and carrots until tender. Drain.

2 Mash cooked potatoes and carrots with the butter and cream, stir in chives and serve.

Serves 4

Smoked Fish Pate

Smoked Fish Pate

150g (5oz) smoked mackerel, skin and bones removed

150g (5oz) smoked trout, skin and bones removed

150g (5oz) smoked salmon, skin and bones removed

90g (3oz) butter

100g (3½oz) natural yoghurt

3 tblspn chopped chives

3 tblspn freshly squeezed lemon juice

½ tspn ground black pepper

1 Blend or process mackerel, trout, salmon, butter, yoghurt, chives, lemon juice and black pepper for 1 minute or until just smooth.

2 Spoon pate into a serving dish and serve with fresh vegetables, cut into bite-size pieces and toast.

Serves 4

Strawberry and Almond Creams

1 punnet strawberries, hulled and sliced

2 tblspn toasted almonds

4 tblspn Grand Marnier

¾ cup thickened cream

1 egg yolk

2 tblspn honey

¼ tspn ground nutmeg

1 Place the strawberries and almonds in a medium bowl, drizzle over Grand Marnier and set aside for 20 minutes.

2 Arrange strawberries and almonds in the bottom of four heatproof ramekins. Whisk together the cream, egg yolk, honey and nutmeg and pour over strawberries and almonds.

3 Grill under low heat for 5 minutes and serve.

Serves 4

77

Lamb Cutlets with Blue Cheese and Pears (bottom), Orange and Fennel Salad

Smoked Trout and Asparagus Terrine

Lamb Cutlets with Blue Cheese and Pears

Orange and Fennel Salad

White Chocolate Mousse

Alternative Main Course: Chicken Saute with Dill and Lemon Sauce

Lamb Cutlets with Blue Cheese and Pears

2 tblspn butter

8 lamb cutlets

50g (1¾oz) cream cheese

50g (1¾oz) blue cheese

1 clove garlic, crushed

½ cup sour cream

2 pears, cored and sliced

1 Melt butter in a large frying pan over moderate heat, add the cutlets and cook for 3 minutes on each side. Transfer cutlets to a warm oven.

2 Blend or process the cream cheese, blue cheese and garlic until smooth, add to the frying pan, stir in sour cream and simmer sauce for 1 minute.

3 Top each cutlet with slices of pear and pour over sauce.

Serves 4

*Smoked Trout and
Asparagus Terrine*

Orange and Fennel Salad

3 oranges, peeled and thinly sliced

1 fennel bulb, sliced

¼ cup walnut pieces

3 tblspn walnut oil

3 tblspn freshly squeezed orange juice

2 tblspn freshly squeezed lemon juice

2 tspn honey

1 Arrange orange slices and fennel slices decoratively on a serving plate. Sprinkle walnut pieces over the top.

2 Dress with combined walnut oil, orange juice, lemon juice and honey.

3 Garnish with sprigs from fennel tops if desired.

Serves 4

Smoked Trout and Asparagus Terrine

3 cups fish or chicken stock

4 tblspn gelatine, dissolved in ¼ cup boiling water

1½ tspn cracked black pepper

1 smoked trout, head, bones and skin removed, broken into small pieces

2 tblspn fresh herbs, chopped

12 tinned asparagus spears, drained

1 In a large bowl, combine the stock with the dissolved gelatine and pepper, set aside and cool to room temperature.

2 Lightly oil four, ¾-cup capacity individual terrine tins or ramekins and pour in the stock to fill a third of the tin. Refrigerate for 1 hour or until set.

3 Place the trout pieces on top of the set aspic, sprinkle the herbs over the top and pour stock to cover, about 1cm (½in) deep. Refrigerate for 1 hour or until set.

4 Lay the asparagus spears on top and cover with the stock to top. Refrigerate for 1 hour or until set. Gently ease terrines out onto serving plates.

Serves 4

Chicken Saute with Dill and Lemon Sauce

Leftovers can be reheated very gently the next day.

6 chicken breast fillets
2 tblspn olive oil
1 small onion, peeled and chopped
75g (2½oz) roughly chopped hazelnuts, lightly toasted
¼ cup chopped dill
600ml (1 pint) hot chicken stock
salt
3 egg yolks
freshly squeezed juice of 2 lemons
250g (½lb) broadbeans, fresh or frozen and defrosted
2 tblspn chopped dill, extra

1 Dry chicken thoroughly on paper towels. Heat oil in a casserole over medium high heat, quickly brown chicken on both sides in 2 batches (see note). Remove from casserole, keep warm.

2 Add onion, saute over moderate heat until softened, about 5 minutes. Return chicken to casserole together with hazelnuts, dill and hot chicken stock and salt to taste. Simmer for 10 minutes or until chicken is cooked through.

3 Meanwhile, lightly beat egg yolks in a small bowl, whisk in lemon juice. Add 3 tablespoons of the simmering liquid to egg yolk mixture, mix in well, then stir mixture back into the casserole. Simmer for another 1 minute, do not boil.

4 Cook broad beans in a separate saucepan, drain and refresh under cold running water. Stir into chicken, allow to heat through for 5 minutes. Serve hot, sprinkled with extra dill.

Note: If fillets at this stage are too crowded in the casserole, they'll sweat in their own juices and will be 'cooked through' long before they brown.

Serves 6

White Chocolate Mousse

White Chocolate Mousse

200g (6½oz) white chocolate
4 tblspn thickened cream
6oz (2oz) butter
3 eggs, separated
75g (2½oz) dark chocolate

1 Combine the white chocolate and cream in a basin over simmering water. Stir continuously until chocolate has melted, set aside.

2 Beat in the butter and egg yolks and place back over the simmering water, stirring constantly until mixture thickens, about 2 minutes. Remove basin from heat and set aside.

3 Beat egg-whites until stiff and fold into chocolate mixture. Pour mixture into serving glasses and refrigerate for 2 hours.

4 Melt the dark chocolate over simmering water and decorate the mousses with the dark chocolate. Return mousses to refrigerate until ready to serve.

Serves 4

When entertaining your guests, why not prepare a few snacks in advance? It makes your welcome so much more relaxed and enjoyable.

GREAT SNACKS, DIPS AND NIBBLES

Prawn (Shrimp) Toast

500g (1lb) cooked prawns (shrimp)

6 spring onions (scallions), chopped

2 tspn grated fresh ginger

2 tspn light soy sauce

½ tspn sesame oil

2 egg whites

6 slices white bread, crusts removed

½ cup fresh breadcrumbs

oil for deep frying

1 Peel and devein prawns, combine in a blender or processor with spring onions, ginger, soy sauce and sesame oil, blend until roughly chopped. Add egg-whites, blend until combined. Spread mixture onto bread slices.

2 Cut each slice into 3 strips. Dip prawn coated side of each strip into breadcrumbs.

3 Deep-fry in heated oil until light golden brown, drain on absorbent paper, serve immediately.

Makes 18

Garlicky Pita Wedges

4 large white pita breads

125g (4oz) unsalted butter, melted

3 cloves garlic, crushed

2 tblspn chopped fresh basil

⅓ cup grated Parmesan cheese

1 Split pita breads in half, cut each half into 4 wedges.

2 Combine butter, garlic and basil, brush over cut side of bread wedges, sprinkle with Parmesan cheese.

3 Place in a single layer on oven trays, bake in a 180°C (350°F) oven for 10 minutes or until crisp.

Makes 32

Spicy Almond and Pecan Mix

¼ cup peanut oil

1½ cups whole blanched almonds

1 cup whole pecan nuts

¼ cup sugar

1 tspn salt

2 tspn ground cumin

1 tspn chilli powder

1 Heat oil in a frying pan, add almonds, pecans and sugar, stir-fry over medium heat until almonds are light golden brown.

2 Remove almonds and pecans from pan, toss in combined salt, cumin and chilli. Cool at least 5 minutes before serving.

Makes 2½ cups

Cheese Biscuits

1 cup self-raising flour

125g (4oz) unsalted butter

60g (2oz) hard blue-vein cheese

2 tblspn freshly grated Parmesan cheese

¼ cup chopped chives

½ cup sesame seeds

1 Sift flour into a bowl, add butter, blue cheese, Parmesan and chives. Knead with fingertips until ingredients cling together and are well combined. Cover with plastic wrap and chill 30 minutes.

2 Roll heaped teaspoonsful of mixture into balls, roll in sesame seeds.

3 Place onto greased oven trays, press out with a fork. Bake in a 180°C (350°F) oven for 10 minutes or until light golden brown. Cool on wire racks. Store in an airtight container.

Makes about 30

Cherry Tomatoes with Herb Filling

⅓ cup slivered almonds

2 punnets cherry tomatoes

125g (4oz) packet cream cheese

1 tblspn chopped fresh mint

1 tblspn chopped fresh parsley

1 tblspn chopped fresh chives

1 Toast almonds in a moderate oven for 5 minutes, chop roughly.

2 Cut top off each tomato, scoop out seeds, reserve 2 tablespoons for filling.

3 Beat cream cheese until smooth, stir in almonds, mint, parsley, chives and reserved tomato pulp.

4 Spoon filling into tomatoes, refrigerate for 1 hour or until firm. Garnish with extra herbs, if desired.

Makes about 36

Tzatziki (Yoghurt and Cucumber Dip)

1 large cucumber

500g (1lb) carton plain thick yoghurt

1 tblspn chopped fresh mint

1 tblspn chopped fresh parsley

2 cloves garlic, crushed

plain corn chips for dipping

1 Peel and coarsely grate cucumber, combine with yoghurt, mint, parsley and garlic. Cover, refrigerate at least 1 hour.

2 Serve with corn chips.

Makes about 2½ cups

DELIGHTFUL SUMMER DINNERS

Light and delicious food is a must for entertaining on warm summer nights. These menus will suit the occasion perfectly.

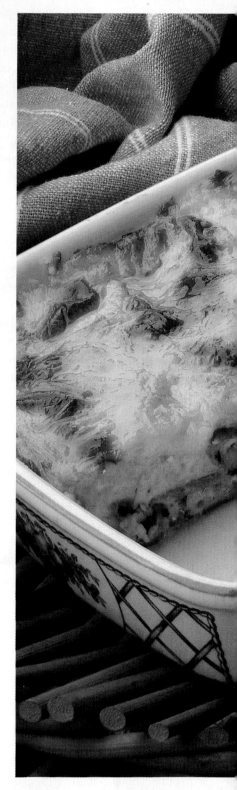

Tomato Picasso

Seafood Lasagne

Warm Fennel Salad with Herbed Cream

Cold Passionfruit Souffle

Alternative Dessert:
Summer Fruit Compote

Warm Fennel Salad with Herbed Cream

3 tblspn oil
2 fennel bulbs, sliced
3 tblspn natural yoghurt
¼ cup sour cream
2 tspn finely chopped parsley
1 tblspn finely chopped chives

1 Heat the oil in a large frying pan over moderate heat, add the fennel and lightly saute for 3 minutes.

2 Arrange on serving plate, top with the combined yoghurt, sour cream, parsley and chives.

Serves 4

Seafood Lasagne

4 tblspn butter
4 tblspn plain flour
2 cups very hot milk
¼ tspn ground nutmeg
1 cup grated Cheddar cheese
spinach lasagne sheets, pre-cooked
750g (1½lb) gemfish fillets, skin removed, cut into 2cm (¾in) cubes
2 tblspn chopped fresh parsley
1 cup grated Cheddar cheese, extra

1 Melt the butter in a large saucepan over moderate heat, stir in the flour, remove from heat. Slowly pour in the hot milk, nutmeg and cheese.

2 Grease an ovenproof baking dish with butter and spread a third of the cheese sauce over the bottom of the dish. Place a layer of pasta on top, place half the fish on top, sprinkle with the parsley and top with another third of sauce.

3 Repeat with remaining pasta, fish and sauce. Sprinkle extra cheese on top and bake in a moderate oven for 40 minutes.

Serves 4

Seafood Lasagne (top),
Warm Fennel Salad with Herbed Cream

Tomato Picasso

Tomato Picasso

---

4 large tomatoes

4 tblspn butter

4 eggs, beaten

4 tblspn cream

1 tblspn finely chopped chives

¼ medium avocado, stoned, cut into small pieces

¼ cup sour cream

---

1 Scoop out the flesh of each tomato and discard.

2 Melt the butter in a large frying pan over low heat. Stir in the combined eggs, cream, chives and avocado and gently scramble eggs, but do not overcook.

3 Spoon mixture into the tomatoes and top with sour cream.

Serves 4

Cold Passionfruit Souffle

---

3 eggs, separated

1 cup sugar

pulp from 3 to 4 passionfruit, sieved

1 cup cream, lightly whipped

10g (⅓oz) powdered gelatine, dissolved in 4 tblspn water

1 cup cream, extra, whipped

½ cup toasted coconut

---

1 Beat the egg yolks with sugar until thick and creamy. Stir in the passionfruit pulp. Fold in the lightly whipped cream and gelatine mixture. Fold in well-beaten egg-whites. Pour into 4, ¾-cup capacity, collared souffle dishes and refrigerate until souffles are set.

2 Remove collars from souffle dishes. Using a small spatula, spread a very thin layer of extra cream around the edge and press toasted coconut into cream. Decorate with cream and passionfruit.

Serves 4

Cold Passionfruit Souffle

Summer Fruit Compote

Vibrantly pretty and effervescent.

1 punnet strawberries
1 large, ripe mango
1 punnet blueberries
300ml (½ pint) fruity white wine
60g (2oz) castor sugar
¼ tspn freshly grated lemon rind
1 clove
thick cream to serve (optional)

1 Hull strawberries, halve if large. Peel mango, cut flesh into cubes. Rinse blueberries, drain well. Combine fruits in a glass bowl.

2 Combine wine, castor sugar, lemon rind and clove in a saucepan, bring to a boil, stirring constantly. Allow to cool, sieve and discard lemon rind and clove. Pour cooled wine mixture over fruit. Cover and refrigerate until ready to serve. Serve with thick cream if desired.

Serves 4

Marinated Prawns (Shrimp)
Wrapped in Bacon

Rack of Lamb with Blueberries
and Mango

Snowpea Salad

Strawberry Ricotta Hearts

Additional Side Dish:
Wild Rice Salad

Snowpea Salad

3 cups snowpeas
1 cup snowpea sprouts
1 red capsicum (pepper), seeded, cut into very thin strips
3 tblspn olive oil
1 tblspn orange juice concentrate
1 tblspn freshly squeezed lemon juice

1 Bring a large saucepan of water to the boil, add snowpeas and cook for 30 seconds, refresh under cold water, drain.

2 Toss the snowpeas, snowpea sprouts and capsicum strips in the combined olive oil, orange juice concentrate and lemon juice.

Serves 4

Rack of Lamb with Blueberries and Mango

2 racks of lamb, 4 chops on each rack
60g (2oz) butter
¼ cup blueberry conserve
2 tspn arrowroot
⅓ cup red wine
1 tblspn brown sugar
⅓ cup chicken stock
½ cup blueberries
mango slices to garnish

1 Interlock racks, cover exposed bones with foil and place in a baking dish.

2 In a small saucepan, heat butter with the conserve until dissolved. Brush over the racks and bake in a moderate oven for 30 minutes or until done, basting regularly.

3 Remove racks from pan and place in a low oven to keep warm while making sauce.

4 Pour off fat from baking dish. Place baking dish over low heat and stir in arrowroot, red wine, sugar and stock, scraping up the bits from the bottom of pan, cook until mixture thickens slightly.

5 Pour sauce through a sieve, stir in blueberries and serve over chops. Garnish with mango slices and serve.

Serves 4

Rack of Lamb with Blueberries and Mango (top),
Snowpea Salad

Wild Rice Salad

The flavour is wonderfully nutty.

75g (2½oz) wild rice

75g (2½oz) brown rice

75g (2½oz) basmati rice

¾ cup chopped fresh chives

2 tblspn chopped fresh parsley

½ cup chopped dried apricots

100g (3½oz) chopped walnuts

DRESSING

2 tblspn walnut oil

2 tblspn olive oil

¼ cup white wine vinegar

juice of ½ a lemon

1 tspn brown sugar

1 tspn mustard

salt

freshly ground pepper

1 Cook rice in separate pots of boiling salted water until al dente. Drain and allow to cool. Combine rice in a salad bowl. Add chives, parsley, apricots and walnuts, mix well.

2 To make dressing: Combine oils, vinegar, lemon juice, sugar and mustard in a screwtop jar. Shake until well combined. Season to taste with salt and freshly ground pepper.

3 Pour dressing over salad, toss well to coat. Serve at room temperature.

Serves 4-6

Marinated Prawns (Shrimp) Wrapped in Bacon

32 king prawns (shrimp), uncooked, peeled and deveined

¼ cup freshly squeezed lime juice

1 clove garlic, crushed

1 tspn grated ginger

2 tspn brown sugar

16 bacon rashers, rind removed

1 Place the prawns in a medium bowl with the lime juice, garlic, ginger and sugar, mix well. Cover and refrigerate for 30 minutes.

2 Cut bacon into strips, about 2cm (¾in) in width and wrap around each prawn. Thread two prawns onto each skewer.

3 Grill under a moderate heat for 2 minutes each side or until cooked through.

Serves 4

Marinated Prawns (Shrimp) Wrapped in Bacon

Strawberry Ricotta Hearts

Strawberry Ricotta Hearts

1¼ cups strawberries, hulled and chopped

¼ cup icing sugar

250g (½lb) ricotta cheese

½ cup thickened cream

10g (2 tspn) sachet gelatine

¼ cup freshly squeezed orange juice

strawberries, for serving

1 Blend or process the straw-berries with the icing sugar, ricotta cheese and cream until smooth.

2 Dissolve the gelatine with the orange juice over simmering water, stir into ricotta mixture.

3 Pour mixture into 4, lightly-oiled, heart-shaped moulds and refrigerate until set.

4 Gently ease hearts out of moulds, serve with fresh strawberries.

Serves 4

Fish Soup

*Warm Chicken and Vegetables
with Red Wine Glaze*

Potato Gratin

Choc-Almond Torte

Alternative Side Dish:
*Mixed Green Salad with
Avocado and Bacon*

Warm Chicken and Vegetables with Red Wine Glaze

12 chicken drumsticks
4 tblspn plum jam, heated
2 large carrots, peeled, cut into batons
1 bunch asparagus, cut into 5cm (2in) lengths
¾ cup broad beans
1 cup chicken stock
3 tblspn redcurrant jelly
½ cup red wine
2 tblspn tomato paste
2 tblspn brown sugar

1 Remove the skin from the chicken and trim knuckles. Brush each drumstick with the plum jam and bake in a moderate oven for 30 minutes, or until cooked through.

2 Bring a large saucepan of water to the boil, blanch carrots, asparagus and broad beans, drain and set aside.

3 Combine stock, redcurrant jelly, wine, tomato paste and brown sugar in a large saucepan over high heat, stir until reduced by half.

4 When chicken is cooked, toss in sauce, with blanched vegetables, serve warm.

Serves 4

Potato Gratin (top), Warm Chicken and Vegetables with Red Wine Glaze

Potato Gratin

4 large potatoes, peeled and chopped

2 tblspn butter

4 tblspn cream

¼ tspn ground nutmeg

1 tblspn chopped parsley

3 tblspn butter, extra

½ cup chopped hazelnuts

½ cup fresh breadcrumbs

1 Boil potatoes until tender, drain. Mash with the butter and cream, stir in the nutmeg and parsley and spoon mixture into a greased ovenproof dish.

2 Melt the extra butter in a medium saucepan, stir in hazelnuts and breadcrumbs. Sprinkle over the potato mixture and bake in a moderate oven for 25 minutes.

Serves 4

Alternative side dish

Mixed Green Salad with Avocado and Bacon

mixed lettuce leaves, washed and dried

2 ripe avocados

juice of 1 lemon

3 tblspn olive oil

125g (4oz) bacon, rind removed, cut into strips, cooked until crisp

1 Arrange lettuce leaves in a salad bowl. Halve avocados, remove stone, peel. Slice and toss in a little of the lemon juice, arrange on lettuce.

2 Combine olive oil and remaining lemon juice in a small frying pan. Warm over medium heat, add crisp bacon pieces.

3 Pour hot bacon dressing over salad, serve immediately.

Serves 4-6

Fish Soup

Fish Soup

3 cups fish stock

½ cup cream

1 cup milk

½ tspn ground nutmeg

seasoning to taste

100g (3½oz) smoked salmon, cut into thin strips

6 chives, cut into 2cm (¾in) lengths

1 Bring the stock to the boil in a large saucepan over moderate heat. Stir in the cream, milk, nutmeg and seasoning. Heat the soup through again.

2 Ladle into warm soup bowls, top with salmon and chives and serve.

Serves 4

Choc-Almond Torte

Choc-Almond Torte

3 egg-whites

¾ cup castor sugar

150g (5oz) ground almonds

3 tblspn cornflour

strawberries for garnish

MOUSSE

2 egg yolks

¼ cup castor sugar

125g (4oz) dark cooking chocolate

2 tblspn Kahlua

⅔ cup thickened cream

1 Beat egg-whites with an electric mixer until soft peaks form. Gradually beat in sugar. Fold in almonds and flour.

2 Grease and line two 23cm (9in) springform pans and divide mixture evenly over each base. Bake in a moderately low oven for 25 minutes. Turn out onto a rack to cool.

3 To make mousse: Combine egg yolks with sugar and beat until creamy, beat in the melted chocolate, Kahlua and cream, cover and refrigerate for 40 minutes.

4 Spread mousse mixture over one of the meringues, top with the other meringue, decorate with whipped cream and strawberries.

Serves 4

Roast Loin of Pork with Coriander Stuffing

150g (5oz) breadcrumbs

2 cloves garlic, crushed

1 tblspn lemon rind

4 tblspn chopped fresh coriander

1 egg, beaten

4 tblspn butter

1.5kg (3lb) boned loin of pork

1 In a medium bowl, combine the breadcrumbs, garlic, lemon rind, coriander, egg and butter, mix well and fill the loin with the stuffing. Roll up and secure with string.

2 Bake in a moderate oven for 1½ hours or until cooked through.

Serves 4

Roast Loin of Pork with Coriander Stuffing (top),
Honey Baked Parsnips and Carrots

Honey Baked Parsnips and Carrots

4 tblspn butter

2 cloves garlic, crushed

2 tblspn freshly squeezed lemon juice

2 tblspn honey

4 carrots, peeled, halved lengthwise

4 parsnips, peeled, halved lengthwise

1 Melt butter in a medium sauce-pan over moderate heat. Add garlic, cook for 2 minutes. Stir in lemon juice and honey, mix well.

2 Place vegetables in a baking dish and brush with the honey garlic butter and bake in a moderate oven for 25 minutes, basting regularly.

Serves 4

Mushrooms Filled with Pate and Bacon

Coriander Soup

Liquid emerald.

1 cup chopped onion

2 tblspn unsalted butter

6 lettuce leaves, preferably outside leaves

185g (6oz) zucchini (courgette), roughly chopped

3 bunches fresh coriander, leaves only

3 cups chicken stock

salt

freshly ground pepper

200g (6½oz) tub, country-style yoghurt or same amount of cream

2 tblspn chopped fresh coriander leaves for garnish

1 In a large saucepan, saute onion in butter over medium heat until just golden, about 5 minutes. Add lettuce leaves, zucchini and coriander, saute 3 minutes.

2 Add chicken stock, bring to a boil, reduce heat, cover and simmer for 20 minutes, or until vegetables are tender. Puree mixture in a processor until smooth. Dilute with water until the consistency is to your liking. Season to taste with salt and freshly ground pepper. Cover and refrigerate until cold.

3 When ready to serve, stir in yoghurt or cream, mix well, check seasoning. Serve cold, sprinkled with coriander. Place any leftover soup in an air-tight container in the freezer.

Serves 6

Mushrooms Filled with Pate and Bacon

4 tblspn butter

250g (½lb) chicken livers, trimmed

4 tblspn port

½ tspn salt

¼ tspn ground pepper

8 large mushrooms, stems removed

1 cup finely chopped bacon, rind removed

1 Melt the butter in a large frying pan over moderate heat, stir in the livers, cook for 2 minutes. Pour in the port, salt and pepper, cook for a further 5 minutes.

2 Blend or process livers and pan juices until smooth.

3 Spoon a little pate mixture into the mushrooms, sprinkle with bacon and cook in a moderate oven for 15 minutes or until bacon is cooked through.

Serves 4

Floating Islands

Floating Islands

6 eggs, separated

½ cup castor sugar

3 cups milk

4 tspn vanilla essence

½ cup castor sugar, extra

toffee for garnish

mint leaves for garnish

1 Beat egg-whites until soft peaks form. Gradually beat in the sugar until dissolved, about 7 minutes.

2 Bring the milk and vanilla essence to the boil, reduce heat to a simmer. Using two dessert spoons, shape spoonfuls of meringue into the milk. Poach for 2 minutes each side. Using a slotted spoon, remove and set aside on paper towels.

3 To make custard: Beat egg yolks and extra sugar until thick and creamy. Gradually pour the poaching liquid into the eggs and beat for a further 3 minutes. Pour mixture into a large saucepan and stir constantly over low heat until custard thickens. Do not boil or mixture will curdle.

4 Serve meringue on a pool of custard. Decorate with toffee and mint if desired.

Serves 4

COLD MENUS FOR HOT DAYS

The dishes in these menus can be prepared ahead, so that you will have plenty of time to spend with your guests.

Chilled Tomato Avocado Soup

Prawn (Shrimp), Avocado and Mango Salad

Salad of Radicchio with Sun-dried Tomatoes and Artichoke Hearts

Summer Pudding

Alternative Main Course:
Smoked Chicken Salad with Watercress and Croutons

Prawn (Shrimp), Avocado and Mango Salad

32 cooked medium prawns (shrimp), peeled, tails intact

2 medium mangoes, flesh cut into thin strips

1 large avocado, flesh cut into thin strips

2 tspn finely grated lime rind

½ tspn fresh chilli, very finely chopped

¼ tspn cracked black pepper

2 tblspn freshly squeezed lemon juice

3 tblspn olive oil

1 bunch dill

1 Decoratively arrange the prawns, mango slices and avocado on a serving plate.

2 Combine the lime rind, chilli, pepper, lemon juice and olive oil, mix well and pour over salad. Garnish with sprigs of fresh dill.

Serves 4

Salad of Radicchio with Sun-dried Tomatoes and Artichoke Hearts

1 radicchio lettuce

1 cup fresh parsley sprigs

200g (6½oz) feta cheese, cut into small cubes

½ cup halved artichoke halves

½ cup sun-dried tomatoes, drained, sliced

1 tblspn freshly squeezed lemon juice

3 tblspn olive oil

1 Decoratively arrange lettuce leaves and parsley sprigs on a serving plate. Arrange the feta cheese cubes, artichokes and sun-dried tomatoes on top.

2 Dress with combined lemon juice and olive oil.

Serves 4

Salad of Radicchio with Sun-dried Tomatoes and Artichoke Hearts (top), Prawn (Shrimp), Avocado and Mango Salad

Smoked Chicken Salad with Watercress and Croutons

2 tblspn unsalted butter

2 cloves garlic, crushed

4 slices toasting bread, crusts removed

2 cups watercress sprigs, rinsed and dried

1 smoked chicken, cut into bite-size pieces

¼ cup vinaigrette

1 Melt the butter in a small frying pan over moderate heat. Add the garlic and cook for 1 minute.

2 Cut each slice of bread into 9 squares and add to the frying pan. Cook on both sides until light golden brown, drain on absorbent paper.

3 Arrange the watercress and chicken pieces on a serving plate. Pour over vinaigrette and toss gently.

4 Arrange croutons on top and serve immediately.

Serves 4

Chilled Tomato Avocado Soup

2 tblspn butter

2 spring onions (scallions), chopped

1 clove garlic, crushed

1 cup tinned tomatoes and juice

2 medium avocados, pitted, peeled and chopped

1½ cups chicken stock

½ cup natural yoghurt

1 tblspn freshly squeezed lemon juice

¼ tspn ground black pepper

1 Melt the butter in a large saucepan over moderate heat. Add the spring onions and garlic, cook for 1 minute.

2 Stir in the tomatoes and avocados, cook, stirring constantly for 5 minutes. Stir in the stock and simmer mixture for 5 minutes.

3 Blend or process mixture with the yoghurt, lemon juice and pepper until smooth. Chill soup before serving, garnish with chives if desired.

Serves 4

Chilled Tomato Avocado Soup

Summary Pudding

10 slices 1-day old white bread, crusts removed

3 tblspn milk

750g (1½lb) mixed soft fruit (raspberries, red currants, blackberries and black currants)

100g (3½oz) castor sugar

1 Lightly grease a 4-cup capacity ring mould or pudding basin. Cut the bread into fingers 3cm (1¼in) wide and moisten with the milk.

2 Place the fruit and sugar in a large saucepan over low heat and bring to a boil, simmer 5 minutes. Spoon off ⅓ cup of the juice as it cools, and reserve.

3 Line the sides and bottom of the mould with the soaked bread slices, reserve enough bread for the top. Spoon the fruit into the mould. Cover closely with the remaining bread. If using a pudding basin, put a small plate over the top and using palm of the hand, press down on the fruit. If using a ring mould, use a spoon to compress. Cover and refrigerate overnight.

4 To serve, place a serving plate over the top and invert. Pour the reserved juice over the pudding, especially where the juices may not have seeped through.

Serves 4

Summer Pudding

Chilled Apple and Fennel Soup

Potato and Mussel Salad with Red Wine Vinegar

Mixed Lettuce Salad

Orange Jellies with Fresh Fruit

Alternative Starter:
Avocado Mousse

Potato and Mussel Salad with Red Wine Vinegar

3 tblspn olive oil

1 onion, peeled and finely chopped

1 clove garlic, crushed

½ cup dry white wine

1 tblspn freshly squeezed lemon juice

2 tblspn sugar

1 tspn oyster sauce

2 tblspn red wine vinegar

2 cups baby new potatoes, cooked, halved

24 mussels, cooked, shells removed

1 tspn chopped parsley

½ cup drained and julienned pimentos

1 Heat the oil in a large frying pan over moderate heat. Add the onion and garlic, cook for 2 minutes.

2 Add the wine, lemon juice, sugar, oyster sauce and vinegar and simmer mixture until reduced by half.

3 Add the cooked potatoes and mussels to the pan and warm through. Stir in the parsley and pimentos and serve warm or at room temperature.

Serves 4

Mixed Lettuce Salad (top), Potato and Mussel Salad with Red Wine Vinegar

Mixed Lettuce Salad

4 cups assorted lettuce leaves

2 pears, cored, thinly sliced

¼ cup walnut halves

1 tblspn tarragon vinegar

4 tblspn walnut oil

1 clove garlic, crushed

1 Arrange lettuce leaves, pear slices and walnuts, decoratively on a serving plate.

2 Pour over combined vinegar, walnut oil and garlic.

Serves 4

Chilled Apple and Fennel Soup

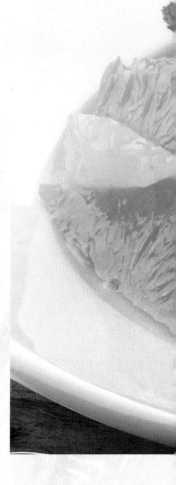

Chilled Apple and Fennel Soup

3 tblspn butter

2 onions, sliced

1 large fennel bulb, sliced

3 green apples, peeled, cored and chopped

1½ cups chicken stock

1 tblspn chopped chives

200g (6½oz) carton natural yoghurt

1 Melt the butter in a large saucepan over moderate heat. Add the onions, fennel and apples, cook, stirring constantly for 3 minutes.

2 Pour in stock, add chives and simmer mixture for 30 minutes or until vegetables are very soft.

3 Blend or process mixture until smooth, stir in yoghurt and refrigerate for several hours or until chilled.

Serves 4

Alternative starter

Avocado Mousse

The creamiest, greenest and purest avocado mousse ever.

4 just-ripe avocados, peeled and stoned

salt

freshly ground pepper

Worcestershire sauce

1 tblspn powdered gelatine

freshly squeezed juice of 1 lemon

2 tblspn finely chopped fresh parsley

2 tblspn finely chopped fresh chives

melba toasts to serve

Orange Jellies with Fresh Fruit

1 Puree avocados in a processor. Season to taste with salt, freshly ground pepper and Worcestershire sauce.

2 Combine gelatine with the lemon juice in a cup, stand cup in hot water and stir until dissolved. With machine running add lemon mixture to pureed avocados.

3 Add parsley and chives, process a further minute. Check for seasoning. Scrape into an oiled, 4-cup capacity ring mould, cover and refrigerate until set, about 2 hours or overnight.

4 Turn mousse out and serve with melba toasts.

Serves 8

Orange Jellies with Fresh Fruit

10g (⅓oz) sachet gelatine, dissolved with 2 tblspn cold water, over simmering water

2 cups freshly squeezed orange juice

2 tblspn Cointreau

1 tspn grated orange rind

whipped cream to decorate

1 tspn orange rind, cut into thin strips, to garnish

fresh fruit to garnish

1 In a medium bowl, combine the dissolved gelatine, orange juice, Cointreau and orange rind.

2 Pour into four, greased, ½-cup capacity moulds and refrigerate until set.

3 To serve moulds, quickly dip the bottom of the moulds into hot water, then ease onto four dessert plates.

4 Top with whipped cream, orange rind and a selection of fresh fruit.

Serves 4

Pimento Soup

Cold Beef Salad with Cornichons

Apricot and Potato Salad

Mango Ice-cream

Alternative Starter:
Smoked Trout Salad with Quail's Eggs

Cold Beef Salad with Cornichons

4 tblspn oil

750g (1½lb) beef eye fillet

2 onions, peeled and sliced

2 cloves garlic, crushed

2 carrots, peeled and chopped

1 bay leaf

1 stalk celery, chopped

4 cups boiling beef stock

DRESSING

½ cup olive oil

¼ cup freshly squeezed lemon juice

1 tblspn chopped fresh thyme

2 cloves garlic, crushed

1 tblspn chopped sage

1 tblspn Dijon mustard

GARNISH

¼ cup cornichons or small, sliced pickles

1 tblspn capers

1 Lebanese cucumber, sliced

1 tblspn red capsicum (pepper), seeded, cut into very small strips

1 Heat the oil at high heat in an electric frying pan, big enough to hold the meat. Add meat and brown on all sides, remove meat and set aside.

2 Add the onions, garlic, carrots, bay leaf and celery to the frying pan and cook for 10 minutes. Return meat to frying pan and place on top of the vegetables. Pour in the boiling stock, cover and cook gently on moderate heat for 2½ hours or until tender. Cool the meat in the frying pan then refrigerate until ready to serve, discard vegetables.

3 Slice cold beef very finely, arrange slices on a serving plate and pour over combined olive oil, lemon juice, thyme, garlic, sage and mustard. Garnish salad with cornichons, capers, cucumber and strips of red capsicum.

Serves 4

Apricot and Potato Salad

500g (1lb) baby new potatoes

¼ cup cream

3 tblspn dry white wine

2 tspn mustard

1 tspn brown sugar

1 tblspn chives, chopped

100g (3½oz) pecan nuts

¾ cup drained and sliced, tinned apricot halves

2 cups watercress sprigs

1 Cook potatoes until tender, cut into bite-size pieces.

2 To make vinaigrette: Combine cream, wine, mustard, sugar and chives in a blender or food processor for 30 seconds.

3 Place vinaigrette in a large bowl, add potatoes, pecan nuts and apricots, toss well. Arrange on a salad plate with the watercress and serve.

Serves 4

*Apricot and Potato Salad (top),
Cold Beef Salad with Cornichons*

Pimento Soup

4 tblspn butter

2 leeks (white part only), sliced

2 cloves garlic, crushed

3 cups drained and chopped pimentos

2 tblspn tomato paste

2 cups chicken stock

1 cup natural yoghurt

½ cup thickened cream

1 Melt the butter in a large saucepan over moderate heat. Add the leeks and garlic and saute for 5 minutes.

2 Stir in pimentos, tomato paste and chicken stock, bring to the boil, reduce heat and simmer for 20 minutes. Cool soup to room temperature, blend or process until mixture is smooth.

3 Stir in the yoghurt and cream and chill for 3 hours before serving.

Serves 4

Pimento Soup

Alternative starter

Smoked Trout Salad with Quail's Eggs

8 quail's eggs or 4 hen's eggs

about 12 mixed lettuce leaves

vinaigrette dressing

125g (4oz) smoked trout, cut into bite-size pieces

brown bread and unsalted butter for serving

dill sauce (see page 12)

1 Bring a large pot of water to a simmer, gently slide in quail's eggs, simmer 3 minutes. Drain, cool under cold running water. Place in refrigerator to cool completely.

2 In a bowl, toss lettuce leaves with a little vinaigrette dressing, divide among 4 entree plates. Peel and halve quail's eggs or quarter hen's eggs, arrange on salad with trout.

3 Serve salad with brown bread, unsalted butter and the dill sauce.

Serves 4

Mango Ice-cream

Mango Ice-cream

flesh of 3 mangos

freshly squeezed juice of 1 lemon

¾ cup castor sugar

2 eggs, separated

1 cup thickened cream

1 Blend or process the mango flesh with the lemon juice and sugar until smooth. Transfer to a tin, cover and refrigerate.

2 Beat the egg yolks until thick and creamy and set aside. Beat the egg-whites until stiff and set aside. Whip the cream until stiff, gently fold in the whipped egg yolks and egg-whites, then fold this mixture into mango puree, cover.

3 Freeze until set or place in an ice-cream maker and process according to instructions.

4 Decorate with slices of fresh mango and strawberries if desired.

Serves 4

HEARTY WINTER MENUS

These tasty and satisfying menus are just right for entertaining on cold winter nights.

Potato Soup with Croutons

Pan-fried Fish

Red Capsicum (Pepper) and
Cucumber Salad

Rhubarb Crumble

Alternative Starter:
Chive Mousse with Parsley
Sauce

Red Capsicum (Pepper) and Cucumber Salad

1 red capsicum (pepper), seeded, cut into thin strips

1 large continental cucumber, sliced

6 button mushrooms, finely sliced

6 black olives, pitted, cut into thin strips

¼ tspn cracked black pepper

2 tspn finely chopped fresh basil

2 tblspn freshly squeezed lemon juice

¼ cup olive oil

1 Decoratively arrange capsicum strips, cucumber, mushrooms and olives on a serving plate.

2 Sprinkle with cracked pepper and basil, pour over combined lemon juice and olive oil.

Serves 4

Pan-fried Fish

2 eggs

6 tblspn thickened cream

½ cup plain flour

4 medium white fish fillets

45g (1½oz) unsalted butter

12 cooked king prawns (shrimp), shelled, deveined, tails intact

lemon for garnish

1 Beat eggs with the cream until well combined. Dust each fish fillet with flour then coat in the beaten eggs and cream.

2 Melt the butter in a large frying pan over moderate heat, add the fish fillets and gently fry for about 4 minutes each side or until cooked through.

3 Serve fillets with fresh cooked prawns and lemon slices.

Serves 4

Red Capsicum (Pepper) and Cucumber Salad (top),
Pan-fried Fish

113

Chive Mousse with Lemon Parsley Sauce

Elegant in its simplicity.

1 bunch chives, roughly chopped

1 thick slice of a peeled onion

½ cup full cream milk

1 bunch chives, extra, roughly chopped

125g (4oz) lite sour cream

2 large eggs

1 tblspn chopped continental parsley

salt

freshly ground white pepper

PARSLEY SAUCE

150ml (¼ pint) thick cream

¼ cup finely chopped continental parsley

juice and grated zest of ½ a lemon

1 Place roughly chopped chives in a processor, process until finely chopped, do not puree. Set aside in a bowl.

2 Combine onion, milk and extra chives in a saucepan, simmer for 3 minutes. Strain milk onto the reserved chives, allow to cool, discard chives and onion in the strainer.

3 Combine sour cream, eggs, parsley and cooled chive-milk mixture in a bowl, whisk briskly to combine. Season to taste with salt and freshly ground white pepper. Spoon into 4 small, buttered ramekins or moulds.

4 Place ramekins in an ovenproof baking dish, pour enough hot water into the dish to come halfway up the sides of the ramekins. Bake in a 180°C (350°F) oven for about 25 minutes, or until set. Remove from the oven, allow to stand at room temperature for about 3 minutes before turning out.

5 Meanwhile, make Parsley Sauce: Combine thick cream, parsley, lemon juice and zest in a small saucepan, heat over very low heat until just warm.

Potato Soup with Croutons

6 Turn ramekins out onto 4 heated entree plates, spoon a little of the Parsley Sauce around mousses. Serve immediately.

Serves 4

Potato Soup with Croutons

3 tblspn butter

1 onion, peeled and chopped

2 cloves garlic, crushed

4 large potatoes, peeled and chopped

1 leek, chopped

3 cups chicken stock

½ tspn ground nutmeg

1 cup cream

4 slices thick white bread, crusts removed, cut into small strips

chopped chives for garnish

1 Melt butter in a large saucepan over moderate heat. Add the onion and garlic, cook for 2 minutes. Add potatoes, leek, chicken stock and nutmeg, simmer over moderately low heat for 20 minutes or until vegetables are tender.

2 Blend or process soup in batches, until smooth. Stir in the cream, mix well. Return soup to saucepan and heat through.

3 Meanwhile, heat oil in medium frying pan over moderate heat, add bread and cook for 2 minutes, turning frequently, serve with soup. Garnish soup with chopped chives if desired.

Serves 4

Rhubarb Crumble

Rhubarb Crumble

4 cups fresh rhubarb, cut into 2cm (¾in) lengths

¾ cup castor sugar

3 tblspn cornflour

1 cup plain flour

2 tspn baking powder

¼ tspn salt

3 tblspn castor sugar, extra

45g (1½oz) unsalted butter, cut into tiny cubes

1 Pour just enough water over the rhubarb to cover, add sugar and gently simmer for 20 minutes or until tender.

2 Dissolve cornflour in ¼ cup water and slowly add to rhubarb, stirring constantly. Continue to cook for a further 3 minutes, spoon rhubarb into four ovenproof dishes.

3 Combine flour, baking powder, salt and sugar in a medium bowl. Stir the cubes of butter through flour mixture then, using your fingertips, rub in the butter until mixture resembles fine breadcrumbs.

4 Spoon topping over rhubarb and bake in a moderate oven for 20 minutes or until golden and crispy.

Serves 4

Leek and Quail's Egg Salad

*Loin of Lamb with Prune
Pinenut Stuffing*

Ratatouille Crumble

Walnut and Spice Pudding

Alternative Main Course:
*Veal Roast with Prosciutto and
Mozzarella Stuffing*

Ratatouille Crumble

¼ cup olive oil

2 cloves garlic, crushed

1 onion, chopped

1 red capsicum (pepper), seeded, cut into 1½cm (5/8in) squares

1 large eggplant (aubergine), cut into 1½cm (5/8in) cubes

1 tblspn tomato paste

3 tblspn white wine

2 tomatoes, cut into 1cm (½in) cubes

¾ cup dry breadcrumbs

¼ cup grated Parmesan cheese

1 tblspn chopped parsley

¼ cup melted butter

1 Heat the oil in a large frying pan over moderate heat. Add the garlic, onion, capsicum, eggplant, tomato paste, wine and tomatoes, cook stirring constantly for 10 minutes.

2 In a separate bowl, combine breadcrumbs, cheese, parsley and melted butter, mix well.

3 Spoon ratatouille into an ovenproof dish. Sprinkle breadcrumb mixture over top and bake in a moderate oven for 20 minutes or until top is golden and crispy.

Serves 4

*Ratatouille Crumble (top), Loin of Lamb with
Prune Pinenut Stuffing*

Loin of Lamb with Prune Pinenut Stuffing

4 tblspn red wine

¼ cup chopped, pitted prunes

¼ cup pinenuts

¼ cup chopped dried apricots

¼ cup ground almonds

1 tblspn chopped fresh parsley

750g (1½lb) boned loin of lamb

1 In a small bowl, combine the red wine, prunes, pinenuts, apricots, ground almonds and parsley, mix well. Set aside to marinate for 30 minutes.

2 Spoon stuffing along the centre of the loin of lamb, wrap up, securing tightly with string.

3 Bake in a moderate oven for about 45 minutes or until cooked as desired.

Serves 4

Alternative main course

Veal Roast with Prosciutto and Mozzarella Stuffing

Any leftovers can be frozen in the meat juices, however, this is best when meat is not sliced. Reheat very gently.

1.5kg (3lb) veal nut, butterflied (see note)

freshly ground pepper

2 tblspn peanut oil

1½ tblspn unsalted butter

salt

¾ cup dry white wine

STUFFING

75g (2½oz) prosciutto, chopped

125g (4oz) mozzarella, roughly chopped

½ cup chopped continental parsley

60g (2oz) freshly grated Parmesan cheese

1 To make stuffing: Combine prosciutto, mozzarella, parsley and Parmesan cheese in a bowl, stir well with your hands to mix.

2 Lay veal nut flat on a work surface, skin side down. Sprinkle inside liberally with freshly ground pepper. Spread stuffing over veal, leaving a 2.5cm (1in) border around the edges. Roll veal into a neat sausage shape, tie securely with string. (If any stuffing is left over, use to stuff some veal scallops in the same manner to cook another time.)

3 Heat oil and butter over medium heat in a casserole dish, preferably oval, so veal will fit snugly. When foam subsides, add veal and brown well on all sides, about 12 minutes. Add salt, turn veal, season other side.

4 Add wine, allow to come to a boil, immediately reduce heat to a simmer, place the lid on top so it does not quite cover the casserole, cook until meat is tender, about 2 hours. Turn veal every 30 minutes in the first hour, every 15 minutes in the second hour, when some of the cheese will ooze out, which makes it more difficult to turn the veal.

5 Remove veal from casserole, keep warm. Add ½ a cup of warm water to the casserole, bring to a boil, scraping up any browned bits from the bottom. Boil until sauce thickens slightly.

6 Slice veal thinly, arrange on a heated serving dish. Spoon the sauce over the meat or serve separately in a sauceboat. Serve immediately.

Note: Ask your butcher to butterfly veal nut for you. This dish is also very good with a veal shoulder, at about half the price. Ask your butcher to bone the shoulder for you, keep the bone for a beautiful gelatinous stock.

Serves 6

Leek and Quail's Egg Salad

Leek and Quail's Egg Salad

12 quail's eggs (see note)

¼ cup olive oil

2 cloves garlic, crushed

2 leeks (white part only), cut into thin strips

1 radicchio lettuce

2 tblspn olive oil, extra

¼ cup French dressing

sprigs of watercress to garnish

1 Bring a large saucepan of water to the boil, add quail's eggs, cook for 3 minutes, drain.

2 Heat the oil in a large frying pan over moderate heat. Add the garlic and leeks, cook for 3 minutes.

3 Arrange the leeks on a bed of lettuce on each entree plate. Shell the eggs and place on top of the leeks.

4 Dress salad with combined extra olive oil and French dressing, garnish with a sprig of watercress if desired.

Note: If quail's eggs are hard to obtain, substitute 3 hen's eggs, hard-boiled, shelled and quartered.

Serves 4

Walnut and Spice Pudding

Walnut and Spice Pudding

75g (2½oz) butter

½ cup brown sugar, tightly packed

1 egg

1 cup self-raising flour

1 tspn ground ginger

¼ tspn ground nutmeg

½ tspn ground cinnamon

¼ tspn ground cloves

¼ cup milk

⅓ cup walnuts, chopped

1 Cream butter and sugar together until light and fluffy. Beat in the egg, then flour and spices, slowly pour in the milk. Stir in the walnuts and mix well.

2 Pour mixture into a well-greased, 4-6-cup capacity pudding basin. Cover with foil then place in a baking dish with 4cm (1½in) of boiling water in the bottom.

3 Bake in a moderate oven for 1½-1¾ hours or until cooked when tested. Turn out pudding and serve with a light hot custard.

Serves 4

Creamy Mushroom Soup

Veal with Apricot Sauce

Pommes Louise

Glace Fig Orange Tart

Alternative Dessert:
Blueberry Brulee

Veal with Apricot Sauce

1 cup dried apricots

1 tspn ground coriander

4 tblspn butter

8 veal medallions

1 Soak the apricots in just enough water to cover for 24 hours. Add the coriander to the apricots and blend or process with the soaking water until smooth. Heat sauce in a small saucepan over low heat.

2 Melt the butter in a large frying pan over moderate heat, add veal medallions, saute for 3 minutes each side or until cooked through. Serve veal with apricot sauce.

Serves 4

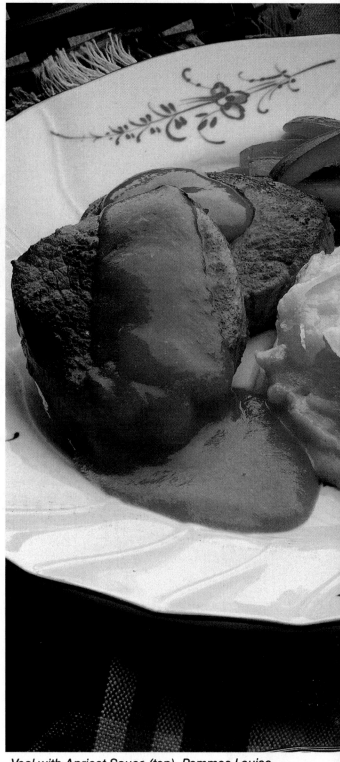

Veal with Apricot Sauce (top), Pommes Louise

Pommes Louise

3 large potatoes, peeled and thinly sliced

2 tblspn butter

2 tblspn plain flour

1 cup hot milk

1¼ cup grated Cheddar cheese

¼ tspn grated nutmeg

1 large onion, peeled and sliced

1 Bring a large saucepan of water to boil, add the potato slices and cook for 5 minutes, drain.

2 Melt butter in a large saucepan over moderate heat, add flour and cook for 30 seconds. Gradually stir in the hot milk and simmer mixture, stirring constantly, until sauce thickens. Remove from heat, stir in the cheese and nutmeg.

3 Arrange a layer of potato slices on the bottom of an ovenproof dish, top with a layer of onion slices, pour over half the cheese sauce. Repeat with remaining potato slices, onion and sauce. Bake in a moderate oven for 25 minutes or until potatoes are cooked through.

Serves 4

Creamy Mushroom Soup

Creamy Mushroom Soup

4 tblspn butter

1 large onion, peeled and sliced

3 cups sliced button mushrooms

1 tblspn chopped fresh chervil

2 cups chicken stock

2 tblspn cornflour

1 cup milk

½ cup thickened cream

1 Melt the butter in a large saucepan over moderate heat. Add the onion and mushrooms, saute for 5 minutes.

2 Add the chervil and stock, simmer for 20 minutes. Blend or process mixture until pureed and return mixture to the saucepan.

3 In a small bowl, mix the cornflour and ¼ cup of milk to a paste, add to the rest of the milk and mix into puree mixture.

4 Cook over moderate heat until soup thickens slightly. Stir in the cream and serve. Garnish with slices of sauteed mushrooms and fresh chervil if desired.

Serves 4

Glace Fig Orange Tart

Glace Fig Orange Tart

250g (½lb) rice biscuits, crushed finely

125g (4oz) butter, melted

1¾ cups glace figs, chopped

1 cup orange juice concentrate

90g (3oz) butter, extra, chopped

2 eggs, lightly beaten

¼ cup pinenuts

1 Combine crushed biscuits with melted butter and press into a 23cm (9in) removeable base flan tin. Bake in a moderate oven for 10 minutes.

2 In a large frying pan, combine figs and orange juice, simmer over moderate heat for 15 minutes. Remove from heat, stir in extra butter and cool for 5 minutes.

3 Quickly stir in eggs and pour mixture into biscuit base. Sprinkle pinenuts over the top and bake in a moderate oven for 20 minutes. Serve with whipped cream or yoghurt if desired.

Serves 4

Alternative dessert

Blueberry Brulee

315g (10oz) fresh or frozen blueberries

2 tspn cornflour

1 tblspn dark brown sugar

150ml (¼ pint) plain yoghurt

150ml (¼ pint) cream

1½ tblspn dark brown sugar

1 tspn cinnamon

1 Place the berries in a saucepan together with a generous cup of water. Bring to a boil, reduce heat and simmer until berries are soft.

2 Remove 2 tablespoons of the liquid from the pan, stir into a smooth paste with the cornflour. Stir back into the pan. Bring to a boil, reduce heat to a simmer, cook for 2 minutes until sauce thickens. Stir in sugar, allow to cool to room temperature. Divide mixture among 4 ramekins.

3 In a bowl, whisk yoghurt and cream until smooth. Spoon over berries, making sure berries are completely covered. Sprinkle with sugar and cinnamon.

4 Place ramekins in refrigerator until well chilled. Then place them in a baking dish with ice cubes packed all around them, under a hot, preheated griller, about 15cm (6in) from the heat, until sugar has caramelized. Return ramekins to refrigerator until sugar has set, serve cold.

Serves 4

Fettucine with Caviar

Beef Fillet with Vegetable Sauce

Potato and Celery Puree

Lemon Delicious Pudding

Alternative Starter:
Spiral Salad with Smoked Salmon and Dill Dressing

Potato and Celery Puree

4 tblspn butter

1 onion, peeled and chopped

2 stalks celery, chopped

4 medium potatoes, peeled and chopped

3 tblspn butter, extra

2 tblspn cream

½ tspn salt

¼ tspn pepper

2 tspn chopped parsley

1 Melt the butter in a large saucepan over moderate heat. Add the onion, celery and potatoes, cook for 5 minutes, stirring constantly.

2 Pour in enough boiling water to just cover. Simmer vegetables until very tender, drain.

3 Blend or process vegetables with extra butter, cream, salt and pepper; sprinkle with parsley and serve.

Serves 4

Beef Fillet with Vegetable Sauce

750g (1½lb) beef eye fillet

6 tblspn butter

1 onion, peeled and finely chopped

1 clove garlic, crushed

1 medium carrot, peeled and chopped into small cubes

1 medium stalk celery, chopped into small cubes

1 cup beef stock

¼ cup red wine

3 tblspn tomato paste

2 tspn brown sugar

continental parsley for garnish

1 Tie eye fillet with string to secure. Melt butter in a large frying pan over moderate heat, add fillet and sear well on all sides. Transfer fillet to a moderate oven, cook for 30 minutes.

2 Add onions, garlic, carrots and celery to the frying pan. Cook, stirring constantly, for 5 minutes.

3 Add the stock and wine to the pan with the tomato paste and sugar, simmer mixture until sauce thickens slightly.

4 When meat is cooked, slice and arrange decoratively on a serving plate, pour over sauce and garnish with continental parsley.

Serves 4

Beef Fillet with Vegetable Sauce (top),
Potato and Celery Puree

Spiral Salad with Smoked Salmon and Dill Dressing

A light starter for a hearty winter dinner.

250g (½lb) pasta spirals

125g (4oz) smoked salmon, cut into strips

12 cherry tomatoes, halved

6 spring onions (scallions), thinly sliced diagonally

1 small onion, peeled and thinly sliced, rings separated

DRESSING

⅓ cup olive oil

3 spring onions (scallions), roughly chopped

juice of ½ a lemon

½ cup tightly packed dill leaves

salt

freshly ground pepper

1 Cook pasta in boiling, lightly salted water until al dente. Drain, rinse under cold running water until cool, drain thoroughly. Place in a salad bowl.

2 Add salmon, tomatoes, spring onions and onion rings to the bowl, toss to mix.

3 To make dressing: Combine olive oil, spring onions, lemon juice and dill in a processor, puree until smooth. Season to taste with salt and freshly ground pepper.

4 Pour dressing over salad, toss to coat. Serve immediately or cover and refrigerate. If refrigerated, allow to return to room temperature before serving.

Serves 4-6

Fettucine with Caviar

Lemon Delicious Pudding

Fettucine with Caviar

300g (10oz) dry fettucine

4 tblspn olive oil

2 cloves garlic, crushed

2 tblspn chopped chives

3 tblspn red caviar

3 tblspn black caviar

2 hard-boiled eggs, shelled, chopped

¼ cup sour cream

1 Cook the fettucine in boiling water until just cooked, drain.

2 Meanwhile, heat the oil in a large frying pan over moderate heat. Add the garlic, cook for 2 minutes.

3 Add cooked fettucine, chives, caviar and egg, toss well and heat through. Top with sour cream and serve.

Serves 4

Lemon Delicious Pudding

60g (2oz) butter

5 tblspn castor sugar

⅓ cup self-raising flour, sifted

grated rind of 2 lemons

juice of 2 lemons

2 eggs, separated

1¼ cups milk

1 Grease a 4-cup capacity ovenproof dish. Cream butter and sugar, add the flour, lemon rind and juice. Beat egg yolks and milk, and mix into the pudding. Whip the egg-whites until stiff and fold in with a metal spoon.

2 Spoon the mixture into the ovenproof dish and place in a baking dish half-filled with boiling water. Bake for 45 minutes until sponge is golden on top.

Serves 4

TEMPERATURE AND MEASUREMENT EQUIVALENTS

OVEN TEMPERATURES

	Fahrenheit	Celsius
Very slow	250°	120°
Slow	275–300°	140–150°
Moderately slow	325°	160°
Moderate	350°	180°
Moderately hot	375°	190°
Hot	400–450°	200–230°
Very hot	475–500°	250–260°

CUP AND SPOON MEASURES

Measures given in our recipes refer to the standard metric cup and spoon sets approved by the Standards Association of Australia.

A basic metric cup set consists of 1 cup, ½ cup, ⅓ cup and ¼ cup sizes.

The basic spoon set comprises 1 tablespoon, 1 teaspoon, ½ teaspoon and ¼ teaspoon. These sets are available at leading department, kitchen and hardware stores.

IMPERIAL/METRIC CONVERSION CHART

MASS (WEIGHT)
(Approximate conversions for cookery purposes.)

Imperial	Metric	Imperial	Metric
½ oz	15g	10 oz	315g
1 oz	30g	11 oz	345g
2 oz	60g	12 oz (¾ lb)	375g
3 oz	90g	13 oz	410g
4 oz (¼ lb)	125g	14 oz	440g
5 oz	155g	15 oz	470g
6 oz	185g	16 oz (1 lb)	500g (0.5kg)
7 oz	220g	24 oz (1½ lb)	750g
8 oz (½ lb)	250g	32 oz (2 lb)	1000g (1kg)
9 oz	280g	3 lb	1500g (1.5kg)

METRIC CUP AND SPOON SIZES

Cup		Spoon
¼ cup = 60ml		¼ teaspoon = 1.25ml
⅓ cup = 80ml		½ teaspoon = 2.5ml
½ cup = 125ml		1 teaspoon = 5ml
1 cup = 250ml		1 tablespoon = 20ml

LIQUIDS

Imperial	Cup*	Metric
1 fl oz		30ml
2 fl oz	¼ cup	60ml
3 fl oz		100ml
4 fl oz	½ cup	125ml

LIQUIDS (cont'd)

Imperial	Cup*	Metric
5 fl oz (¼ pint)		150ml
6 fl oz	¾ cup	200ml
8 fl oz	1 cup	250ml
10 fl oz (½ pint)	1¼ cups	300ml
12 fl oz	1½ cups	375ml
14 fl oz	1¾ cups	425ml
15 fl oz		475ml
16 fl oz	2 cups	500ml
20 fl oz (1 pint)	2½ cups	600ml

* Cup measures are the same in Imperial and Metric.

LENGTH

Inches	Centimetres	Inches	Centimetres
¼	0.5	7	18
½	1	8	20
¾	2	9	23
1	2.5	10	25
1½	4	12	30
2	5	14	35
2½	6	16	40
3	8	18	45
4	10	20	50
6	15		

NB: 1 cm = 10 mm.